# PRACTICAL BOAT CANVAS WORK

## LISA CARR

*WATERLINE*

Published by Waterline Books
an imprint of Airlife Publishing Ltd
101 Longden Rd, Shrewsbury, England

ISBN 1 85310 567 8

A Sheerstrake production.

A CIP catalogue record of this book
is available from the British Library

Typeset by Servis Filmsetting Ltd
Printed in England by Butler & Tanner Ltd, Frome and London.

# Introduction

If you have ever looked around a marina or harbour and admired a sail cover, awning or bimini top; appreciated the ease with which an entering yacht drops and stows its sails or enjoyed a visit to friends in a cool, insect-free saloon – and then thought to yourself, 'Can I have all this?' . . . then this book is for you.

You will find many useful ideas which can be adapted to fit your boat to make it easier to handle and more comfortable to sail. The diagrams are easy to follow and step-by-step instructions simplify each project. You will find details of the items needed for each task and photographs demonstrate the finished results, so I hope that it will be of use to any practical boat owner.

Everything in this book has been tried and tested by the author and in the appropriate conditions – and they all work! The financial savings that can be made if you *do-it-yourself* are considerable, but the sense of achievement is even greater.

Best of Luck

Lisa Carr

This book is for Jeannie – who started me writing,
for Mary-Jo – who encouraged me
and for Shackle – who has helped and suffered by reading each paragraph at 3am.

Thanks, my friends.

# Contents

# Sewing Machines and How to Use Them

Everything in this book can be made with a fairly heavy-duty domestic sewing machine which can take a No14 or 16 needle. (You will also need a sailmaker's palm and needles for thicker corners and stitching on webbing.) It does not necessarily have to be a purpose designed sailmaker's machine, although a model such as the '*Reed's Sailmaker*' is a worthwhile investment. Buy it from the manufacturer or from a reputable source, since I have experienced purchasing a machine with a false label which proved totally inferior to the genuine model it purported to be.) The older 'Singer' machines can be found in second-hand shops and are entirely suitable. If you are shopping for a machine, carry a sample of the sailcloth that you will be working on and insist on a demonstration to see it is up to the job. To sew sails, you will need to be able to use a No14 or 16 needle and increase the foot pressure to the maximum weight.

Provision for a hand-crank is a must, but if you have a generator on board (240V or 110V), it is worth getting the equivalent motor. Finding a 12V motor can be difficult but the '*Jabsco Water Puppy*' water pump motor will fit most, if not all, domestic machines. Carry spare belts, spare needles and spare bobbins with you. In the case of the last two, they should be kept in an airtight container with a drop of machine oil to prevent rust.

Having a sewing machine on board and knowing how to use it, is a way of earning money while you are cruising; practise on your own sails first though! There are many yachts that do not have the space for a sewing machine and whose owners are only to happy to find someone to repair their boat canvas.

The machine should be oiled well at all times and when not in use protected by a waterproof cover. It should be stowed in a dry locker and secured against the movement of the boat.

# Stowaway Lazy Jacks

*What you will need*

5mm braidline
5mm shock-cord
9 nylon/plastic snap-hooks
6 nylon/plastic/stainless-steel thimble eyes
2 small blocks
2 stainless-steel saddle-eyes
3 slides (for the attachment points under the boom)
1 or 2 small cleats
1 small stainless-steel shackle

*The mainsail has just been dropped and lies tamed and contained within the lazy jacks*

Lazy jacks originated in the old clipper ships. When the crew was reduced by scurvy, desertion or drowning, it became necessary to find a simpler way of lowering and stowing the heavy sails.

Nowadays, lazy jacks provide an easy way of controlling a mainsail or mizzen as it is dropped – especially for the single-hander or short-handed crews.

If lazy jacks are left in position when sailing, the lines are likely to cause severe chafe on the sailcloth and particularly to the seam stitching. If the lines are unhitched from the end of the boom and taken forward to the mast, then the dangling loops of cord risk becoming caught in the mast winches or fouling the halyards.

There are many variations on this theme; some are complicated and expensive to install, some can cause chafe on the sails and stitching and some look good but prove to be either ineffective or not suited to your sail. As is so often the case, the old traditional methods can be adapted and improved to create a system that will work for you – and this system is easy to make.

Stowaway lazy jacks work on the principle of tension through shock-cord attachments, allowing the lines to be stowed parallel to the mast when released from under the boom. They remain ready for immediate use on short passages but can be easily removed for long distances when the sail will be set for a day or more.

This simplified design uses two small blocks, one fastened to the underside of each spreader, a third of its length out from the mast. (If you have double spreaders, use the upper set.) The blocks should be attached by shackles to saddle-eyes, riveted or through-bolted, underneath the spreaders.

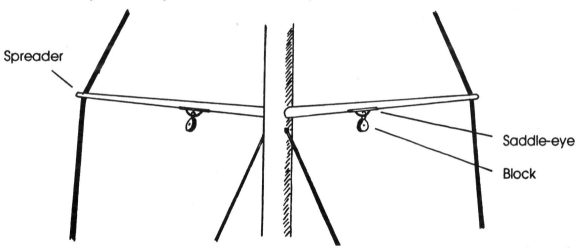

**Fig 1**

The measurements are simple if you have a sail-plan; alternatively you may have to go up the mast to measure the distance between spreader and boom.

Using graph paper, draw the mast and boom to scale and at right angles. Divide the boom into quarters and draw a line between the spreader and the quarter mark nearest the outer end of the boom (Fig 2).

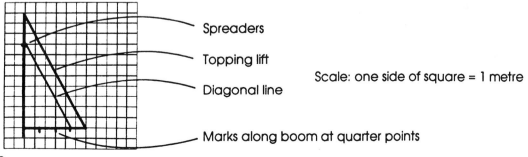

Spreaders

Topping lift

Diagonal line

Scale: one side of square = 1 metre

Marks along boom at quarter points

**Fig 2**

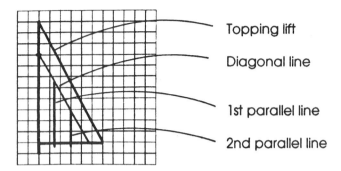

**Fig 3**

Parallel to the mast, draw light lines to join the first and second quarter marks on the boom to a position vertically above them on the diagonal. (Fig 3)

Mark a position on the diagonal that is half-way between the point where the first vertical light line cuts and the spreader. Then mark another position on the diagonal that lies half-way between the

points where the two light lines cut. Draw lines between these two new half-way points on the diagonal and the quarter marks on the boom. (Fig 4)

This will give you the maximum catchment at the bulk of the sail, although you can still fine-tune by moving the slides below the boom.(See photo)

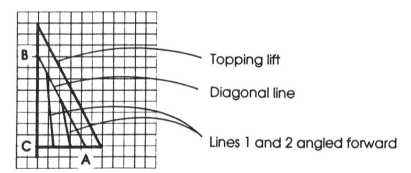

**Fig 4**

*The sliding eye under the boom can be moved for final minor adjustment.*

To calculate the length of line required for the uphaul (A–B) and the downhaul (B–C), measure it on your graph paper and then cut two lengths of line the total length of A–C. Seal one end of each with a hot-knife or soldering iron and stitch or whip a nylon/plastic thimble into the other ends. (Fig 5)

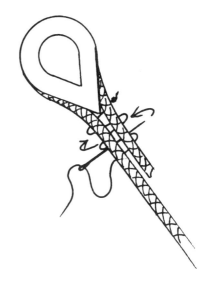

**Fig 5**

If you are confident of your graph paper measurements, continue. But if you wish to see the overall effect in reality, then mark out the true dimensions on the ground in either chalk or by utilising a length of line such as a sheet. If using a rope line, weight the head, tack and clew (making sure that the angle between mast and boom is a right angle) with something like a brick or sleeping crew. Use strips of tape to mark the spreader height (B) and the critical under-boom attachment points 1, 2 and 3 onto the line. There is also one other important measurement, the height of your sail cover, taken between the underside of the boom to the top of the mast collar – this will prevent the tensioning shock-cord from exposure to the damaging ultra-violet rays of the sun when the lazy jacks are not in use.(Fig.6)

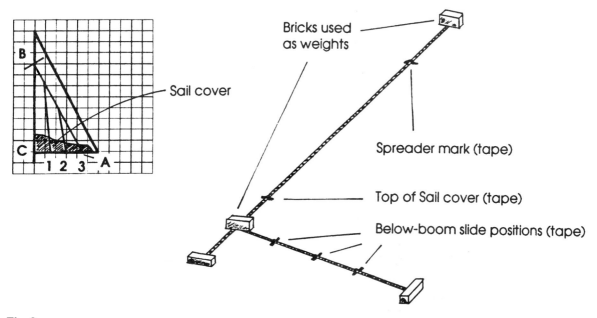

**Fig 6**

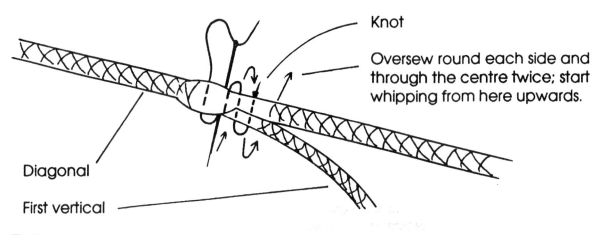

Knot

Oversew round each side and through the centre twice; start whipping from here upwards.

Diagonal

First vertical

**Fig 7**

Tie the lower ends of the two diagonal lines together through the thimble eyes, and lay them down the mast so that the eyes sit just below the mark for the head of the sail cover. The cut ends should come up the mast to the 'spreader' point and down the other side. Weight them down at the 'spreader' and mark them both with indelible marker pen at this point.

If you have not chalked in the diagonal line on the ground, tie a light cord through both thimbles and pull them in a straight line from the 'spreader' to No 3 mark on the boom. Using the graph (See Fig 4) for the measurements, mark on the diagonal the attachment points for the vertical lines. You will need four of these, each with a thimble at one end. To avoid wasting rope, it is easier to tie two light lines onto the diagonal, one at each mark. Bring the diagonal forward to the mast again to give you the position for the other four thimbles (both sets of three should be level and just below the head of the sail cover.), and the approximate lengths of rope you will need.

Cut four lengths of braidline long enough for the two pairs, but allowing extra to go round the thimbles and be seized.

Replace the diagonals at No 3 and attach the upper ends of the other two pairs at their respective marks on the diagonals. This can be done by neatly melting the upper ends slightly and rolling them in your fingers (wetted) until the ends are pointed and stiff. They can then be inserted into the core of the diagonal (point upwards) at the marks, and be stitched and whipped in place. (Fig 7)

Re-lay the three pairs of lines down the mast and using the thimbles already in the ends of the diagonals as a guide, seize in the other two pairs, trimming off any excess line. (Fig 5)

Lay the lines in their 'finished' position to the marks on the boom, each pair tied together, with a thin line leading down to its mark. (You may need to apply weights on the diagonal at the attachment points to keep it straight.) (Fig 8)

In this position you can see more clearly how to calculate the lengths of lines needed for your mast and the height of your sail cover. When all the lines are laid together, the thimbles should all be almost level.

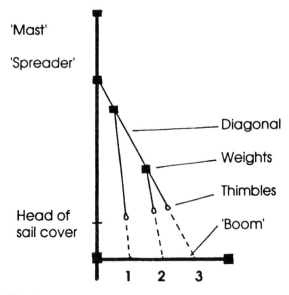

'Mast'

'Spreader'

Diagonal

Weights

Thimbles

'Boom'

Head of sail cover

1  2  3

**Fig 8**

## Shock-cord Tensioning Lines

For these it is worth buying good quality shock-cord with a minimum of 2-1 stretch. (To check, measure 25cm unstretched and then pull it out to its maximum; it should expand to 50mm or more.) Marlow is a well known brand which is found in most chandleries.

To ascertain the lengths required, measure from the thimble on each line to the centre point below the boom at the corresponding mark and then add 30cm. Ask the chandler to cut it with a hot-knife. Alternatively, you can melt the ends to seal them yourself, but do this outside in the open air as the fumes are quite unpleasant.

Thread a nylon/plastic snap-hook onto each length and stitch and whip one onto each end. Find the centre of each length and fasten the loose hook at this point. Stitch through the doubled-over shock-cord close to the hook, round it and through three times each side, then three times round at right angles to separate the two halves. (Fig 9)

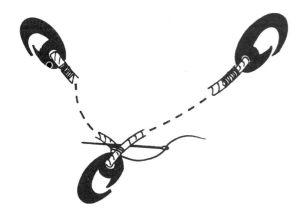

**Fig 9**

Providing that you have internal track under the boom that will take sail slides, fitting the lazy jacks is straightforward. Insert three slides into the track and lock each one into position, either with a self-tapping screw just forward of it (inside the track) or with stoppers such as those used to keep the mainsail luff slides in the mast track. If you have a solid boom you may have to experiment to locate the exact position for the hooks before permanently attaching the three saddle-eyes required.

It is a good idea to mark each shock-cord tensioner with a matching mark on the corresponding thimble (or the line just above it). This can be one bold stripe of indelible marker pen for number one, two for the centre and three for the diagonal.

Pass one end of each shock-cord under the boom and hook both ends to their matching thimbles. Make sure that the centre hooks are level with each other and hanging free under the forward end of the boom..

Installing the lazy jacks is simple; all you do is to get up the mast to the spreaders and pass one free end of the rope through each block, bringing both ends down together. Once through the blocks, tie the ends together with an overhand knot (which can be easily undone if you need to adjust the lines, or remove them completely during a winter lay-up.)

Hook the centre of each shock-cord to its slide or saddle-eye, and take up the lines until the marks on the diagonal are at the spreader blocks. Make off the lines and try the catchment – you may need to adjust it either by loosening or tightening the lines.

When not in use, unhook the below-boom attachments, and the lazy jacks will lie neatly either side of the mast. When you need them just pull back and hook on. (If you have a boom-vang you will need to unhook one side of number three and pass it behind before re-hooking it.)

To remove the lazy jacks completely, stitch a 'mouse' – a light line –long enough to reach up to the spreaders and back down to the boom, to tie the cut ends and pull these back through the spreader blocks. Cut the mouse free and make it off. This will enable you to re-install the lazy jacks without the need to go aloft.

Combine this system with a 'simple sail stower' for easy mainsail handling.

*As the sail descends it is captured between the lazy jacks and is under control at all times.*

*When the sail is lashed to the boom, the lazy jacks can be unclipped and stowed at the mast.*

# A Simple Sail Stower

*What you will need*

Shock-cord
Nylon/plastic snap-hooks
Tape measure, waxed thread and a needle

*This system of mainsail stowage is simple to make and use. It saves the endless search for sail-ties which are somehow never to hand when you need them most.*

If you have to drop a sail in a hurry and find your-self with both arms full of billowing Dacron and desperately need at least one sail-tie to subdue it, try this solution.

For each sail stower you will need some 6mm–8mm shock-cord of 2 – 1 stretch. The size and length will depend on the size and weight of the sail to be tamed. For a mainsail you will require six plastic snap hooks and for a headsail thirteen.

## Mainsail or Mizzen Stower

Measure the boom and cut the shock-cord to twice this length. Thread one hook on and tie it in the centre with an overhand knot. (Fig 10)

Thread five hooks, facing the same direction onto one half of the shock-cord, pushing four towards the top. The last hook is the attachment at the aft end of the boom. This is fixed in place by threading the end of the (unhooked) shock-cord through the hole in the opposite direction and stitching the two ends together. (Fig11)

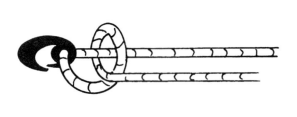

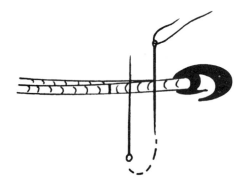

**Fig 10**

**Fig 11**

Hook each end out to hold the shock-cord taut but not stretched and mark them at 25%, 50% and 75% of the length. Using a heavy darning needle (or small sail needle) and waxed thread, stitch and seize the two lengths together at these points, with a hook between each join. (Fig 12)

Hook one end to the goose neck or fitting below (or to a cord loop if the snap will not fit) and the other attaching hook to the aft end of the boom. If you have a boom vang or a mainsheet

block forward of the clew end of the boom, hook the sail stower to one side of both and make the seizings as near to these points as possible.

The sail stower will lie neatly under the boom, out of the way but ready for instant use.

Drop the sail, stow it loosely on the boom and, holding it with one elbow, reach over and snap the hooks onto their corresponding lengths. The shock-cord will automatically adjust to hold the sail snugly. (Fig 13)

**Fig 12**

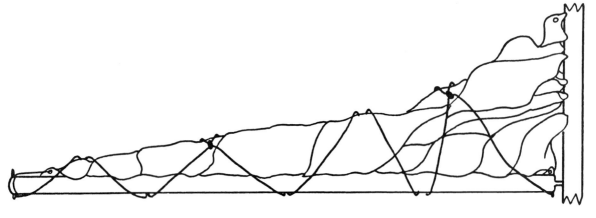

**Fig 13**

*Here the headsail is stowed clear of the deck – keeping it clean in the dock and with space beneath to let heavy seas wash over the deck without pulling the sail overboard.*

## Headsails

The same system can be used for genoas or jibs by using additional hooks on the other half of the shock-cord to fasten it to the top lifeline. This method will keep the sail out of the way, off the deck and avoids any chance of it becoming damaged by warps or anchor chain. In the case of a yacht with twin forestays, it enables you to have a second sail ready to hoist at a moments notice.

For headsails use shock-cord two-thirds the length of the foot of your largest genoa, double this measurement and fasten the forward hook in the centre as before. Thread five hooks onto one length, six onto the other with the final hook at the end of both lengths as with the mainsail version. Measure the half-way point and seize the third of the five hooks to this mark, catching both lengths of shock-cord together, making sure that there are three hooks each side of the join on the other length. (Fig 14)

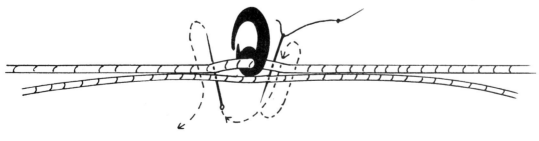

**Fig 14**

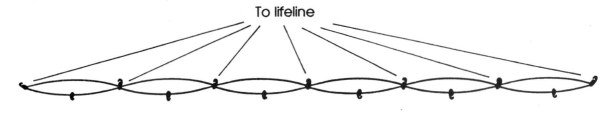

To lifeline

**Fig 15**

Space the hooks evenly on the lifeline length and seize them to both lengths of shock-cord, so that there is one free-sliding hook between each join. (Fig 15)

Attach the forward hook to a point on the pulpit and as near as possible level with the forestay. Take the aft hook to a point aft of a stanchion to keep the shock-cord taut and snap the intermediate hooks to the top lifeline.

Drop the genoa, loosen the sheets, fold one third of the foot forward and tuck it into the bulk of the sail. Fasten the hooks to the matching shock-cord around the sail and over the lifeline. (If you have netting around the foredeck, stretch the shock-cord round the sail. It will stay in place.)

# Sail Protection

The worst enemy of any sails is the sun. As a rough guide, every month that they are left exposed to the UV rays will take a year off their life. So sail covers and sailbags are a necessity, but if yours falls to pieces and you cannot find or afford a replacement from a sailmaker, why not try your hand at making it yourself?

### Sail Covers
To make a sail cover you need a few basic measurements.
You will also need a sewing machine, zig-zag stitch and/or straight-stitch (or endless patience) and the following items:
Sewing shears
An office-size stapler
Tape measure
Tailor's chalk
Graph paper
Sail cover hooks and eyes (or hooks and grommets).
3mm cord (braided leech-line is ideal).
Two short lengths of Velcro™.
Double-sided tape.

*Good protection against the sun for the mainsail – but what about the human skin?*

First, stow the sail on the boom as you would normally, not too neat a stow or your cover will end up being too tight. Then, following Figure 16, fill in the measurements.

A) Height from top of sail to underside of boom.

B) Measurement around the mast. (Including halyards if you wish to leave them on.)

C) Length of boom from centre front of mast to end of sail.

D) Measurement around the boom. (Make sure that there is 5cm of boom from the end of the sail to enable the collar to sit neatly.)

E) Measure 50cm back from the centre of the mast and then measure around the sail and under the boom; divide this measurement in half.

F) Measure back another 50cm and do the same.

G) At the clew of the sail do the same.

H) At the head of the sail, where the headboard sticks out, do the same. This measurement should be on the loose side otherwise the headboard can wear through the cover.

Take a piece of graph paper and draw Figure 16 to scale, adding 3cm to the bottom of the hem and 5cm to the front hem and reducing the collars to 1cm. Your drawing should then look like the wrong side in Fig 17. Now you need to know what type of material and how much of it you will need.

The best material to use is acrylic, sold under various trade names of which Yachtcrillic™, Sunbrella™ and Tempotest™ are probably the best known and easily available. It is a man-made fabric, guaranteed UV resistant for five years, washable and water resistant; but it breathes, unlike PVC which, when used for a cover, can cause condensation and therefore encourage mould spots on the sail. Acrylic comes in various widths – choose the widest available for fewer joins.

Make two cut outs of your drawing, draw to the same scale the width of your material and lay the cut outs on it as in Figure 16. (If measurement 'A' is greater than the width, as in Figure 18.) Then

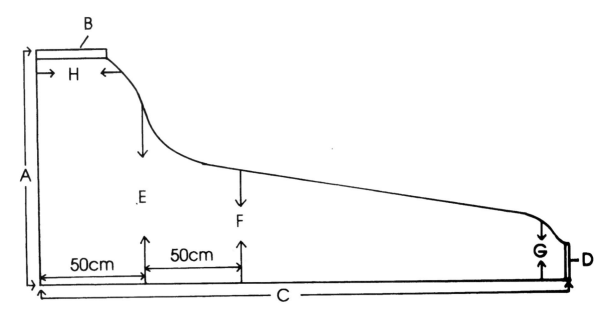

**Fig 16**

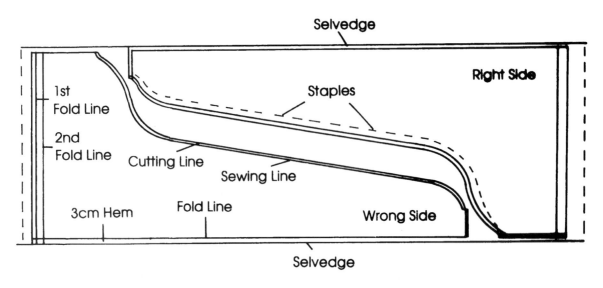

**Fig 17**

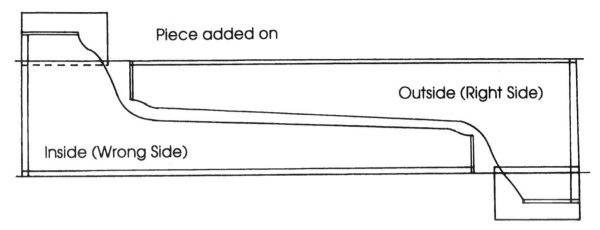

Piece added on

Outside (Right Side)

Inside (Wrong Side)

*Fig 18*

measure the total length required (not forgetting that in Figure 18 you will have to get extra for the added-on parts), convert it back to metres and go buy your material.

In the same way that you did it on the graph paper, make the first drawing onto the cloth with tailor's chalk. This can easily be erased if you make a mistake. Mark the sewing line and allow 1cm seam allowance outside this – this is the cutting line. Cut along this line, pick up the piece and turn it so that the selvedge matches the opposite side (See Figure 17). Then staple the two pieces together, far enough inside the sewing line for the machine foot to avoid the staples.

If measurement 'A' is greater than the width of the cloth it will be necessary to add the extra piece (See Figure 18) to both sides before cutting and stapling. When you have added the piece to the first side, cut and reverse it. You will now see where the extra material is required to be added on the second side.

If your stapler will not reach far enough inside the stitching line, trim off excess material to match the first side. You will then be left with a long strip, slightly on the bias. Reserve this for the mast and boom collars. (See Figure 19)

Turn the sewing machine to straight-stitch and sew down the stitching line. If you have a hot-knife (or soldering iron) run it down the line of the cutting edge to seal it, making cuts towards the stitching line at the inward curves. Remove the staples. Now, starting from the narrowest end, spread the cover open, right side up, and stitch (preferably with a wide zig-zag) down just to the right of the seam, over the seam allowance. This makes for a neater finish and although the exposed thread will perish faster, the first line of straight stitching will hold the cover together as it is not exposed to the sunlight.

Then turn under the 3cm hem along the bottom selvedges and sew it down with two rows of stitching. For the front, turn under 1cm and under again by 4cm and stitch twice. (These hems can be pressed down with a warm iron or stapled to keep them in place for sewing.)

For the mast collar, take measurement 'B' and add 12cm to the length. Cut a strip this length and 15cm wide, sealing one long edge with a hot-knife. Place the other edge against the edge of the cover where it goes round the mast, right sides together, pulling the body of the cover straight to match the collar. Sew along the stitching line (See Figure 20). Turn the collar up,

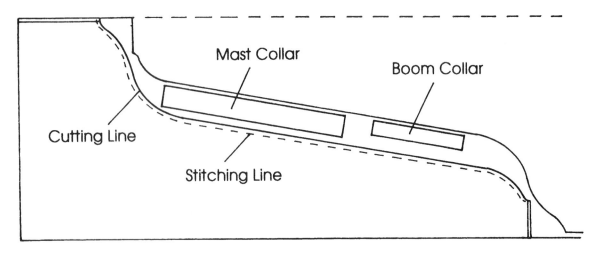

Mast Collar

Boom Collar

Cutting Line

Stitching Line

**Fig 19**

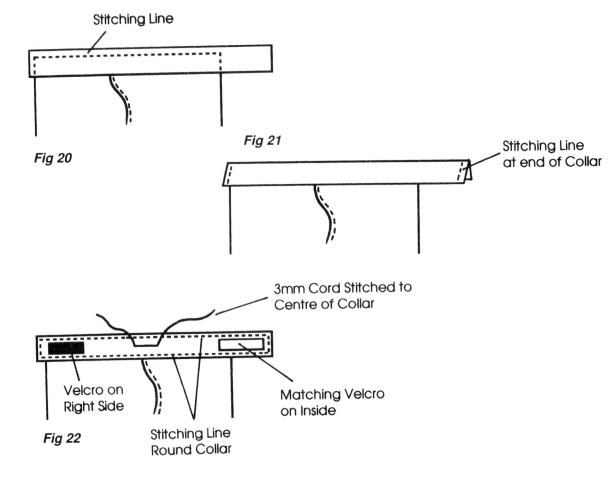

Stitching Line

**Fig 20**

**Fig 21**

Stitching Line
at end of Collar

3mm Cord Stitched to
Centre of Collar

Velcro on
Right Side

Matching Velcro
on Inside

**Fig 22**

Stitching Line
Round Collar

pressing the seam allowance towards it. Then fold it back on itself and stitch the ends (See Figure 21). Now turn it right side out and, matching the sealed edge of the first line of stitching, crease the top edge with your finger and staple (or iron) it to hold it in place while you sew round the collar.

Cut a piece of Velcro the length of the overlap and sew one part to the overlap on the wrong side and the other part to the collar on the right side. Take a length of 3mm cord two and a half times the measurement of 'B' and stitch it to the centre of the collar. (See Figure 22) For the boom collar, follow the same method, but make the width 9cm instead of 15cm.

An alternative method of fastening the cover round the mast and boom is to add 7cm to the top and end of your cut out material (instead of 1cm for the seam allowance). This should, for the mast be parallel to the selvedge; and for the boom at right angles to it. (A collar round the mast looks neater and is as easy to fasten.)

When you have stitched the hems on the front and bottom (See Figure 23), turn in 1 cm at the top and end, and then in 3cm and sew along the inner edge only. Thread the correct length of cord (2Ω times the measurement) through the hem, matching the ends, and catch the cord with needle and thread at the seam line to prevent it pulling out. This will give you a 'drawstring' effect.

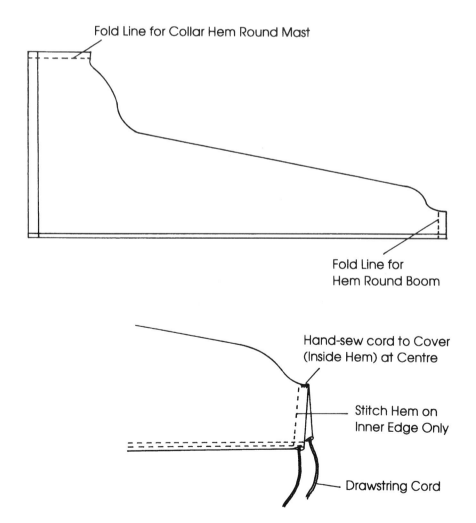

Fold Line for Collar Hem Round Mast

Fold Line for Hem Round Boom

Hand-sew cord to Cover (Inside Hem) at Centre

Stitch Hem on Inner Edge Only

Drawstring Cord

*Fig 23*

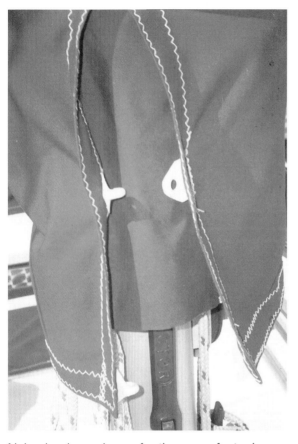

Nylon hooks and eyes for the cover fastenings

back and forth a couple of times on each one. On the front they need to be about 30cm apart and on the bottom about 75cm–100cm apart, starting from 20cm aft the mast.

Some people prefer to use sew-on hooks on one side of the cover with pairs of grommets on the other and a length of cord or shock-cord threaded through. The disadvantage of shock-cord is that it will eventually lose its elasticity when exposed to long periods of sunlight. Another method is matched eyelets on both sides of the cover and a single lacing through, but this is time consuming to fasten, as are sewn on ties. It is also possible to use 'turnbuttons' but I would not recommend these since the backing plate has sharp edges which will easily cut through the fabric and pull out. Anyway, any metal snaps will eventually corrode and need replacing – however, the choice is yours.

Your cover is now ready for fitting. If you have winches or a mast ladder on that part of the mast that must be covered, then provision must be made to allow for them either by cutting holes or adding extruded covers.

For a mast ladder, the rungs of which are best left exposed, measure the height and width of the step and cut a rectangle of cloth 10cm longer and wider. Then mark on it the exact size of the step, in the centre and on the wrong side of the fabric patch. Then seal the edges of the patch with a hot-knife. Mark the outline of the step onto the cover and place the patch onto this, right sides together and matching the outline of the step. Cut the centre (See Figure 24) then turn the facing to the inside and stitch it down twice around – once close to the hole and then around the edge of the facing.

Now you have to decide how you want to fasten the cover. There are several alternatives. The easiest method (and probably the most durable) is to use sew-on hooks and eyes made of nylon; your sailmaker should be able to supply you with these. A normal sewing machine should be able to stitch through the flat plate of nylon to attach them to the cover. You will need to sew

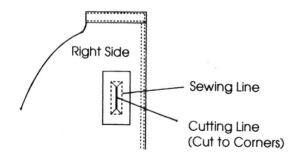

**Fig 24A**

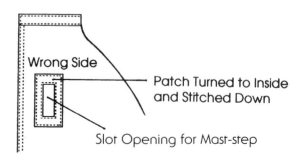

**Fig 24B**

Follow the same procedure for winches using a circle instead of a rectangle if you wish to leave them exposed. However, if you want to keep them under the cover and the sail-cover is not loose enough to fit comfortably over them, you will have to add an extrusion.

Firstly mark the exact centre of the winch on the sail-cover.

Then for your extruded winch cover, measure round the base and measure the height of the winch and cut a rectangle of material to this size, plus 2cm for seam allowance. Use $\pi^2$ to find the radius of the circle or if you are not mathematically minded measure around a plate, bowl etc. of nearly the same circumference. Then cut a circle of cloth and stitch it to the side piece *before* you sew up the short side.

By using this technique, you can present it to the winch to make sure it is not too small. It should not fit too tightly because the sail cover itself will hold it in place and it will need to be a little manoeuvrable. When you have ascertained

that the fit is satisfactory (and this should be done with the fabric inside out), match the short edges together, mark the sewing line and then stitch along it. Turn the cover right side out and check again that the fit is satisfactory.

Mark a circle on the sail-cover, using a compass or the like, to position the cover. Draw another circle 1cm inside the first to provide your cutting line. Notch the seam allowance to just inside the first circle that becomes the stitching line. (See Figure 25)

Run a band of double-sided tape around the right side of the winch cover base to hold it in place for sewing. On the inside, mark a line on the base 1cm up from the raw edge as a sewing guide-line. To fit the cover for stitching it will be more convenient if you fill it with paper to give it its correct shape. Now peel off the protective paper from the double-sided tape and push the cover through the hole from the right side until line A meets line B. (See Figure 26).

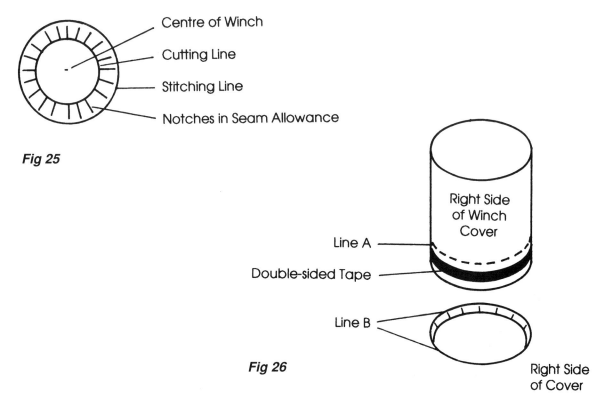

Centre of Winch

Cutting Line

Stitching Line

Notches in Seam Allowance

**Fig 25**

Line A

Double-sided Tape

Line B

Right Side of Winch Cover

Right Side of Cover

**Fig 26**

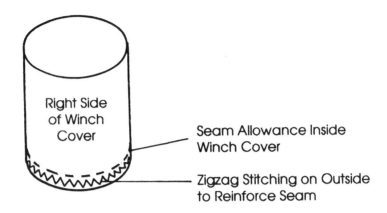

Right Side
of Winch
Cover

Seam Allowance Inside
Winch Cover

Zigzag Stitching on Outside
to Reinforce Seam

*Fig 27*

Press the notched seam allowance against the double-sided tape, turn the sail-cover over and carefully straight-stitch along the line inside the winch cover. Press the seam allowance up into the winch cover and zig-zag stitch it from the outside. (See Figure 27)

That's about all there is to it unless you want to add your boat's name along the cover. The quickest way to do this is to cut the letters from insignia cloth. (Usually available from sailmakers in white, red or blue.) It is best to adjust the lettering and spacing between letters before you commit the self-adhesive insignia material to the cover.

Ensure the name will appear in a neat horizontal line. It is best to practise drawing the characters of the alphabet that you will need on paper before cutting the rather expensive sticky back material. If you do not have an artistic bent it is better to use capital letters only. If you are an artist you will not need me to tell you what imaginative and distinctive lettering and designs can be used. Figure 28 may be of some help.

Most insignia material is better if it is ironed on (gentle heat) after its initial application. Do this as you would have done before the invention of the steam iron to press a pair of pants – ie lay a damp cloth over the cover and numbers before ironing.

You will now have a sail cover that you can be proud of because it looks good and because you made it yourself. It will be easy to put on and take off so it is worth using whenever the sail is not in use. The protection it affords should add years to the life of your mainsail. Try not to let sun or rain awnings rest on the sail-cover as they may chafe through where they meet.

**SE A  E ᴀGL E**

How not to do it. The letter spacing is uneven and the characters have been cut to uneven sizes.

**SEA EAGLE**

Capital letters evenly spaced and level. Looks good.

***FAST LADY***

Italic capitals suggest speed and match the name.

*Fig 28*

# Sail Bags

*What you will need*
Strong nylon material
2 No 1 brass or stainless grommets
3mm braidline
2cm wide nylon or polyester webbing
Tailor's chalk, pins, an iron, straight edge and tape measure.

*A strong and sensible sailbag that is easy to make*

These should be large enough in width and depth, to hold a loosely packed sail.

If you leave a headsail hanked onto the forestay overnight or for any lengthy period, it should be bagged to protect it from UV and flying grit or dirt. With a suitable bag you can quickly stuff the clew in first (with sheets still attached and left protruding from the bag's mouth) followed by the bulk of the sail, pulling it up to the forestay where it can be secured and tied down by tightening the drawstring and making it off on the forestay with a quick-release knot. The carrying handle on the base of the bag can then be tied to the upper lifeline to hold the bag and sail clear of the deck. The halyard can be left attached and also secured by the drawstring.

This will mean that the headsail is ready for instant use in an emergency situation but looks neat and you have the confidence that you are protecting your sail.

Most sailbags that you buy or that come with the sail are made with a circle of cloth as a base sewn onto the body of the bag. The weight of the sail inside often causes that seam to split. For a stronger bag (and one that will fit more easily through a hatch) it is simpler to make it from one piece of cloth, with a square base.

If your hatch is not large enough to pass a sailbag through or if you do not stow the sails below, then it is better to have a shorter and wider bag that will make sail packing easier. Measurements will vary according to the size of the sail; however the finished size should be large enough for the sail to fit fairly loosely inside.

Take a length of cloth that measures the circumference of the finished bag and wide enough for one and a half times the required height. Fold it in half along the length and straight-stitch down the side and along the bottom. (See Figure 29)

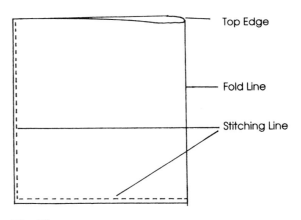

**Fig 29**

For added strength press the seam allowances over and from the right side zig-zag stitch along it a little to the side of the seam. Do not worry if you cannot sew right to the corner as this will not show.

Measure the bottom of the bag and divide by two. Crease the fold line or mark it with chalk. With the bag inside out, fold it across the corners, matching the bottom seam to the crease at one side and to the side seam at the other. Pin the seam lines and folds in place. (See Figure 30)

Take your halved measurement (for example we shall assume that it is 50cm) and, using a ruler or straight edge, measure 25cm each side of the centre seam to the fold. (See Figure 31)

Mark this line and stitch along it, tying off the ends.Fold the corners to the middle, where they should meet if the bag is to be a perfect square. Stitch round them as in Figure 32.

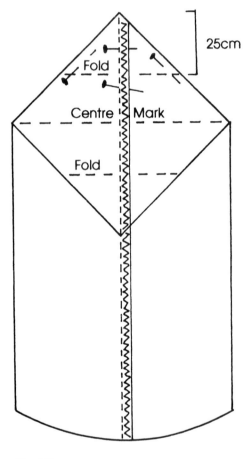

**Fig 30**

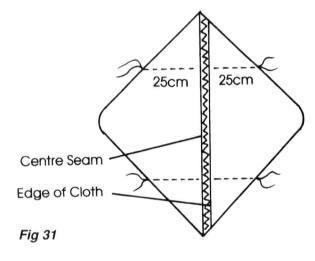

**Fig 31**

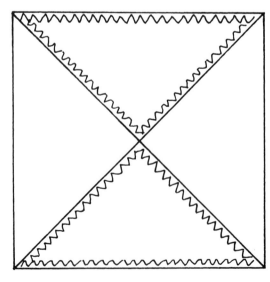

**Fig 32**

For the drawstring at the top, mark a line round the bag 1cm from the edge and another line 4cm down from the first. Cut a patch 10cm by 4cm and lay it on the inside of the bag with the long side touching the second line and stitch round it. This will reinforce the grommets through which the drawstring emerges. Mark the position for the grommets (No 1 size) 6cm apart and 1cm down from the top of the patch and insert them. (See Figure 33)

Crease along the first fold line round the bag, then along the second one. Run the cord in through one grommet, round the bag and out through the other grommet and then knot the ends together. Push the cord to the top of the hem so that it will not catch in the machine and pin the hem down. Stitch along the bottom of the hem. (See Figure 34)

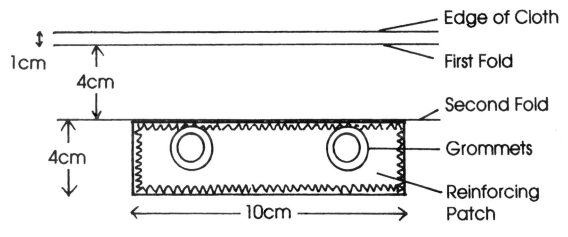

Edge of Cloth
First Fold
Second Fold
Grommets
Reinforcing Patch

1cm
4cm
4cm
10cm

**Fig 33**

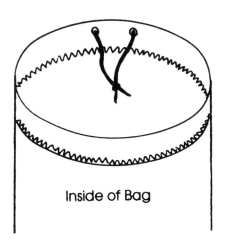

Inside of Bag

**Fig 34**

*A strong webbing handle on the base of this sailbag.*

There are various ways of attaching a handle to the base of the bag.

1) The strongest handle is made by putting in a grommet at the centre of each triangle. Measure the distance between them and cut a strip of 2cm wide webbing to this length plus 15cm. Push the ends of the webbing through the grommets from the outside, taking care that it is not twisted, until you have 7cm emerging from each. Pin each end down away from the centre and stitch them in place. (See Figure 35)

2) It is possible to use rope through the grommets, rather than webbing. Either tie the two ends together inside the bag or put a stopper knot at each end to stop them pulling through the grommets. This method does however, put a lot of strain on the grommets and they may pull out.

3) Webbing can simply be stitched to the base on the outside, but in this case you have no drain holes in the bottom of the bag in the event of having to stow a wet sail.

Any of the above methods can be used to make a side handle, but you will need to sew a reinforcing patch onto the inside of the bag first.

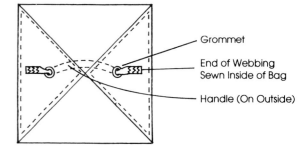

Grommet

End of Webbing
Sewn Inside of Bag

Handle (On Outside)

**Fig 35**

If you stow your sails below via a deck hatch, the bag can be made to fit by taking the measurement of the hatch opening and cutting the cloth to that length. In this case you will need to increase the height of the bag. Stitch as before, but for the corners use the measurements of two opposite sides. This way, if your hatch measures (for example) 55cm by 40cm you will end up with a rectangular base. Depending on which measurement you choose for the corners, they will either have a distance between them (Figure 36a) or overlap (Fig 36b).

To add that professional touch, you should consider marking the name of the sail that the bag will contain clearly on the outside. Using a waterproof marking pen and a stencil cut for fairly large letters, you can indicate if it contains for example 'NO 1 GENOA' or 'STORM JIB'. The practical aspect of this is self evident if you have guest or new crew aboard and adds to safety if you are unfortunate enough to be scrabbling about searching for the storm sails in rough conditions.

While on this topic another useful addition is the boat's name. It not only looks seamanlike, but may also prevent someone mistaking your sail for another if it happens to be in a sail loft or in storage somewhere.

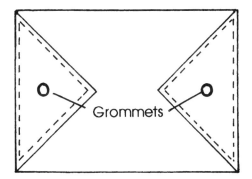

**Fig 36A**

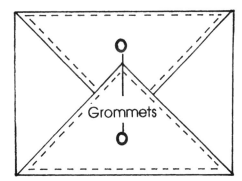

**Fig 36B**

*The sailbag contains the sail which is still hanked to the forestay. The sail is therefore protected, ready for use and is clear of the deck.*

## Sacrificial Strips – Roller-Furling Headsails

A roller furling headsail that is left hoisted (and furled) for most of the time, other than in use, requires some form of protection from UV degradation and airborne pollutants often found on the dockside and near ports. This protection can either be in the form of a 'sleeve' or 'sock' hoisted up over the sail, or more usually a 'sacrificial strip' stitched onto the sail and made from some form of UV resistant material.

In considering the fabric to use for the strip you should bear in mind the weight of the sailcloth from which your sail is made. (Either your sailmaker can tell you or you should know if you have made the sail.) Because the strip is attached to the leech of the sail, un-necessary weight is not desirable since in lighter airs it will tend to distort the aerodynamic shape of the sail. Therefore select a cloth weight that is below the weight of the sailcloth itself; the sacrificial strip bears no deliberate load and is there for protection only.

There are several sailcloth manufacturers who make UV retarding (Note not UV proof) sailcloth and also fabrics specially woven for other marine purposes where strong and prolonged exposure to UV can cause problems – bimini tops and awnings for example. It is best to seek advice on what is available, then you can also decide if you want your strip to be in colour, often dark blue (said to be less UV absorbent than other colours) but which you may consider does not enhance the appearance of the sail when set, or alternatively a fabric that matches as closely as possible the colour of your sail – often a creamy cotton colour.

It is easy enough to attach the strip yourself, though you may have to hand stitch through the head, clew and tack panels if you do not have access to a heavy duty sewing machine.

To work out how much material you will need, measure the length of the leech and divide this measurement by the width of the cloth. This will give you the number of strips to cut. For the width of the strips (from selvedge to selvedge) measure (at right angles to the leech) the exposed cloth when the sail is rolled and then add 10cm. Do the same for the foot of the sail,

adding 5–8cm (depending on how tightly you furl it). Cut the strips across the width with a 'hot-knife' or flat bladed soldering iron to seal the edges, using a straight-edge rule or a metal strip to ensure an even cut.

When sewing the strip in place, make sure that you are applying it to the exposed side! The easiest way is to mark the clew when the sail is furled.

Starting at the head, lay the first strip down the leech, (if necessary pushing the leech-line to the centre of the tabling or hem) and stitch it as close to the edge as possible. Approximately 2cm before the selvedge, slide the next strip underneath and stitch over it; this will allow for the curve of the inverse roach and ensure that the inner edges of the strips will overlap. (See Figure 37)

Continue with each strip until you reach the clew. If your machine cannot handle the reinforced patches, these are not too difficult to do by hand. If the leech-line exits from a grommet and is made off to a cleat, trim the cloth so that it will lie neatly around these. (See Figure 38)

For the strip at the foot, slide the first panel just underneath the inner edge of the last leech panel, again aligning it with the edge. (See Figure 39)

Since the foot is likely to have an outward curve, the overlap at the edge need not be quite so much.

If you are not too sure of the shape of your sail, it may pay you to lay it out on a flat surface and place your strips onto it before you start sewing. In this case, you could stick them in place first to ensure that you get the correct tension.

Once you have stitched down the outer edge of the leech and the foot as far as you can by machine, it is advisable (both for extra strength and better shape) to over stitch the inner edge of the tabling. This will make the strip lie flatter and therefore easier to stitch down on the inner edge. If the leech strip is much wider than the 'arm' of your sewing machine, it is better to run a line of stitching down the centre of the strip before machining the inner edge. (See Figure 40)

Sew the inner edge in place, making sure that the tension of the strip matches that of the sail. Turn the sail round and stitch each join, being

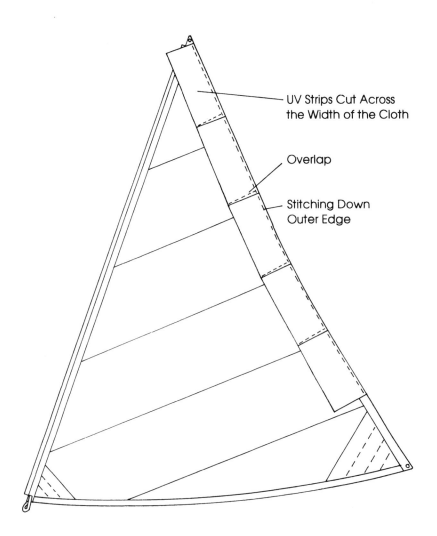

UV Strips Cut Across
the Width of the Cloth

Overlap

Stitching Down
Outer Edge

**Fig 37**

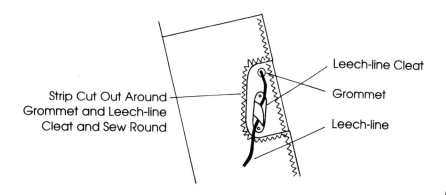

Strip Cut Out Around
Grommet and Leech-line
Cleat and Sew Round

Leech-line Cleat

Grommet

Leech-line

**Fig 38**

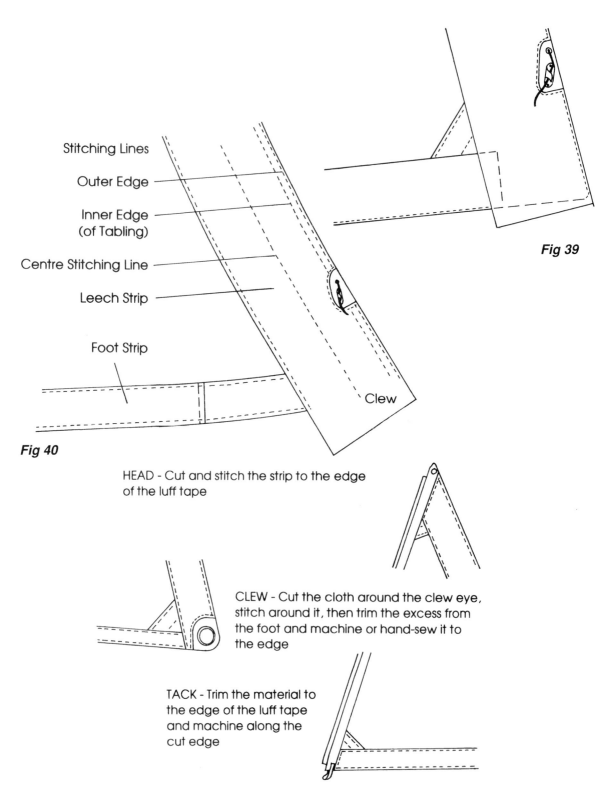

Stitching Lines

Outer Edge

Inner Edge
(of Tabling)

Centre Stitching Line

Leech Strip

Foot Strip

Clew

**Fig 39**

**Fig 40**

HEAD - Cut and stitch the strip to the edge
of the luff tape

CLEW - Cut the cloth around the clew eye,
stitch around it, then trim the excess from
the foot and machine or hand-sew it to
the edge

TACK - Trim the material to
the edge of the luff tape
and machine along the
cut edge

**Fig 41**

careful to leave enough space at the leech tabling for the leech-line to pass freely.

At the head, clew and tack, trim off the excess material and either hand or machine stitch around the edges. If you have to hand stitch the outer edges of the strip through the reinforcement patches here, use a cross-stitch, if necessary by punching holes first with a spike or nail. (See Figure 41)

When the leech and foot strips are sewn in place, it is worth the extra time to reinforce them with a loosely curved line of stitching from edge to edge, head to clew and clew to tack. (See Figure 42)

If you are unlucky enough to damage the sacrificial strip, this stitching will prevent the wind from getting underneath and tearing the strip from the sail, which could cause further damage to both.

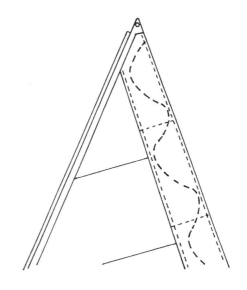

**Fig 42**

*Bad protection – areas of sail are left exposed*

*Good protection – the entire sail is protected*

37

# Bimini Top

*What you will need*
Stainless-steel (or aluminium) tubing, hinges and fastening plates

UV-resistant material
No 1 grommets
Saddle-eyes
4mm cord
Open-ended zipper
2.5cm wide webbing

To make your own bimini, you will first of all need the frame to support it. This can be made from aluminium tubing, but stainless-steel is better as it is stronger and will not corrode in a salt-laden atmosphere. The frame should be designed to offer the maximum shade possible, but low enough to clear the boom.

*This easily made bimini top provides ample shade. This design is particularly useful on boats where the main boom does not run very far aft above the cockpit.*

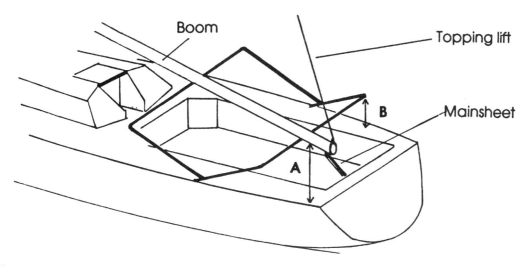

Boom

Topping lift

B

Mainsheet

A

**Fig 43**

Hoist the mainsail and swing the boom to one side so that it is above the edge of the cockpit. Measure this distance – A, subtract 5cm and this will become the height of the frame – B. (Fig 43)

Tie a line from the mast to the backstay to mark the height and fasten a light pole across this line, tied to the backstay and down to the lifeline at each end, making sure that it is level. Decide on the point where the frame will be attached to the boat; about half-way along the cockpit side is ideal, but make sure that it will not interfere with the sheet winches or other running rigging. The frame can be fastened either onto a plate mounted flat onto the cockpit coaming or onto a fitting on the side of the cockpit. (Fig 44)

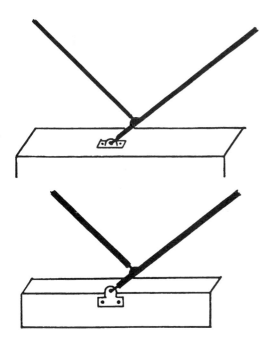

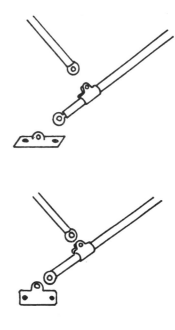

**Fig 44**

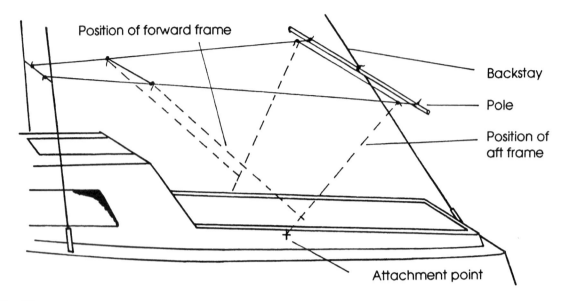

**Fig 45**

Tie a rope between the aft main shrouds, below the level of the boom, at the same height as the pole on the backstay. Fasten a light line between the pole and the rope on each side, above and parallel to the sides of the cockpit. Two cords tied between these lines in the position of the fore and aft bimini frames will enable you to measure the length of the sides. (Fig 45)

The corners of the frames should be bent in identical curves. If you do not have the use of a pipe-bender, it is advisable to take the pipe, the frame dimensions and a template of the curves to a professional, who would also be able to make up the hinged brackets shown in Fig 44.

Once the attachment points are screwed or bolted firmly in place, fasten the frame on loosely. (Not forgetting to slide the attachments for the forward frame on first.) Now join the forward frame to the aft one. As long as the bolts are not tightened too much, both frames should remain adjustable in all directions. When they are in the desired position, it is worth hoisting the mainsail to confirm that the boom and sheets are clear and that the finished bimini will create the maximum area of shade. Once satisfied, tighten all the bolts and to hold the frame while you make the top, tie a line from a handrail on the cabin roof to the forward frame and another from the aft frame down to a suitable point on the aft

deck or transom.

Now for the top. The best material to use is UV-resistant acrylic – your sailmaker should be able to supply this. It comes in a variety of colours and widths – the wider the better as your bimini will have a neater fit if you can make it from a single piece. If you have to join it, the seam should be at the centre from fore to aft.

Take the measurements for the length at the greatest distance between the frames and for the width from just over the curve on both frames. Add to the length 40cm and to the width 10cm. Cut the material to these dimensions and turn over 5cm hems at each side along the length, stitching them down twice (at the inner and outer edges).

If you cannot seal the raw edges with a hot-knife or soldering iron, turn it under 1cm before stitching.

With the hemmed edges together, crease the fold to mark the centre of the cloth. Make a chalk mark 20cm back from the forward edge on the crease – this will show where the centre front of the cloth meets the centre of the forward frame.

Lay the material over the frames, matching these points and the back crease to the centre of the back frame. Starting at the centre front, fold the spare material under the frame and pin it in place from the top. Then move to the back and do the same, making sure that the centres match and the material is stretched tight. Move along 20cm and pin again. (This is easier if you have someone to help, one at each frame , as you can then see instantly if one or other of you is pulling the cloth too tight or if it is not lying straight.) When you have pinned both ends in place, the cloth should be smoothed and unwrinkled. If it is not, keep adjusting the pins until you have a good fit. (Fig 46)

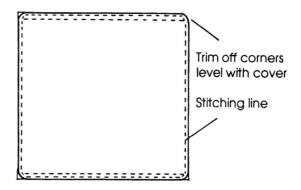

*Fig 48*

Trim off the corners level with the edges of the cover and turn the top over again. Check that the sleeves are the same width all along (if not, trim them until they are) and turn the curved edges over 1 cm towards the top, clipping the curves so that they lie flat. Stitch the hems down.

Press the seam allowance at the join between sleeve and main cloth towards the sleeve and from the other side run a line of stitching along (close to the seam) to hold it in place.

Fold the sleeve to the inside, creasing along the seam. At the half-way point of each curve make a mark and insert a grommet, across the seam. This is where the support lines for the frames will emerge. (Fig 49)

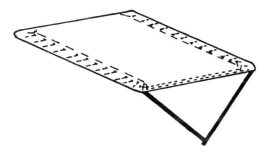

*Fig 46*

Using tailor's chalk, draw a line along the front of the forward frame and along the back of the aft one. Un-pin the cloth and lay it down with the chalk marks upwards. Straighten the line if necessary and cut 1 cm outside it. You will be left with two long strips which will form the sleeves. (Fig 47)

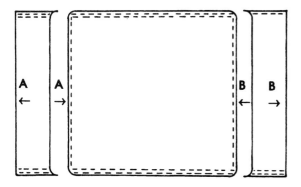

*Fig 47*

Turn each cut-off piece over and place them on top of the main cloth, matching the hems at each side and the long edges, A to A and B to B. Pin or staple them together. Turn the cloth over and stitch 1cm inside the cutting line of the cover. (Fig 48)

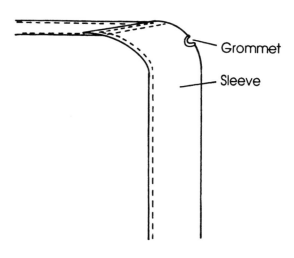

*Fig 49*

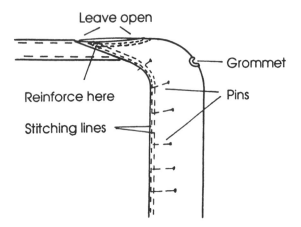

**Fig 50**

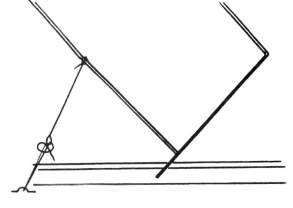

**Fig 51**

With the seam creased flat, pin the curved (inner) edge of the sleeve to the top and stitch it down, on the hemmed edge and 1cm inside this, reinforcing the ends. (Fig 50)

The bimini frame needs to be tied down at each corner; at the back it can be to the corners of the pushpit and at the front to the stanchions or to saddle-eyes screwed onto the cabin sides, which will provide freer access to the cockpit and side-decks. The support lines should be angled slightly outwards to keep the top tight on the frames.

Measure these distances and cut the lines (4mm braided cord is ideal) half as long again. Tie one loosely at each far corner of the front and back frames (so that you can adjust them once the top is in place). Undo the support line between the frames, loosen the bolts slightly on the far side, and undo the bolts on the near side so that the frames will separate to allow the bimini top to be slid on. Push the top onto the frames towards the centre, and re-bolt the frames together and in place. Tie the near side support lines on and feed all four lines through their respective grommets.

Slide the top along the frames in both directions until the curves of the cloth are over the bends in the frames. Tie the back two lines down evenly, then take the tension on the front lines until the top is stretched tight and flat in all directions . (The best method of tensioning the lines is to tie a loop 20cm up from the attachment point,

take the free end round this point, back through the loop and pull it down until the cover is taut enough; then tie it off. (Fig 51 )

If you want side curtains for the bimini, it is advisable to have them detachable, since the top will be in use most of the time, and the sides will only be necessary when the sun is low. In fact you only need one curtain which can be attached on either side depending on the direction of the sun. Although if you are to spend time in crowded anchorages or marinas, a curtain on both sides will offer greater privacy.

To make the curtain(s), measure the distance along the hem of the top between frames to find the length and from the hem to just short of the lifeline for the width. If you like, for extra shade, you can angle the forward width forward of the bottom edge. (Fig 52)

Add a hem of 4cm onto all four sides, turn these over and stitch down twice all round. Mark the centres of the top and bottom hems and put in grommets here and in each corner. Mark the corresponding positions on the side hems of the top and either sew by hand short lengths of cord here, or take the top down and put in grommets to match the ones in the curtain. (If you are only making one side curtain, it will be wrong side out on the other side of the boat.) The grommets at the bottom edge will need lines attached to fasten the curtain to the lifelines.

If the mainsheet traveller is at the forward end of the cockpit, you may be able to create more

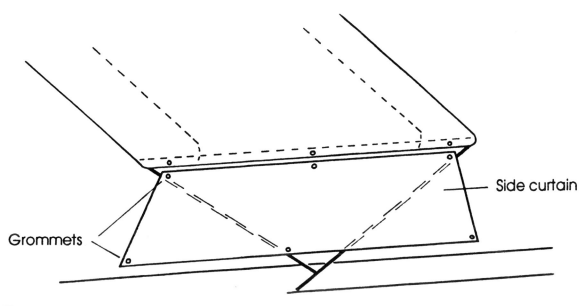

**Fig 52**

shade if the back frame is aft of the backstay. In this case, when the frame is tied in position measure the distance between it and the stay and mark the cloth on the centre crease at this point. Remember to add to the measurement the 20cm extra for the sleeve. Cut along the crease to this mark and then 5cm further.

Fit the top as before, and cut off the sleeve allowance, making sure that the cutting lines are matching. To allow for any movement or adjustment to the top and to avoid it chafing on the backstay, cut out a 10cm long by 5cm wide

opening from the inner mark towards the back. (Fig 53)

To finish off the slit edges along the crease, cut two strips of cloth 5cm wide and the length of the slit (less the 10cm cut out). If you cannot cut these from the selvedge of the material, seal one edge of each with a hot-knife or soldering iron. Lay the raw edge of each strip to the cut edge along the crease and stitch 1cm in from the edge. Press these strips towards the centre, fold them over the raw edges to the inside and stitch them down. (Fig 54)

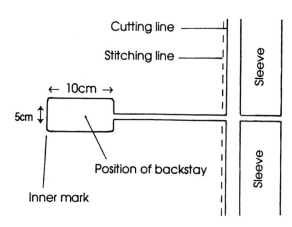

**Fig 53**

**Fig 54**

Do the same for the cut edges at the sleeve centre, then attach the two halves of the sleeve as before, putting in the grommets for the support lines. Mark along the edge of the other half as a guide line; you will need to put in an open-ended zipper here made of heavy-duty plastic, the length of this half of the sleeve.

To reinforce the cut out, take a length of 2.5cm webbing, fold it in half, slide it over the cut edge and sew it in place. (It will be easier to tack it on first so that the edge of the cloth is well up into the fold of the webbing.) At each end reinforce the stitching and trim off the spare webbing with a hot-knife or soldering iron.

To fit the zipper for the other half of the sleeve, lay one edge of it (with the puller towards the outer edge of the bimini and the joined end at the centre) along the guide-line and stitch it into place. Press the sleeve over, and turn the edges under where it meets the teeth on the other half of the zip. (You may have to trim off any excess material inside and clip the curves so that it lies flat.) Pin it onto the zip, separate the two halves and stitch the zipper firmly to the sleeve. (Fig 55)

Insert a grommet at each side of the centre back and on the seam to tie the ends together, plus three on each side of the centre split on the reinforcing cloth to enable you to join the two halves aft of the backstay.

Open the zip and slide the bimini onto the frame from the opposite side. Bring this side round the backstay, fasten the zipper round the frame and attach the grommets together with short lengths of light cord. Tension the frame with the support lines until the top is evenly stretched, and – enjoy the shade.

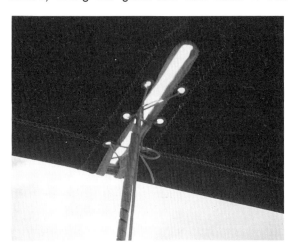

*Here the backstay runs up through the slit in the back of the bimini top.*

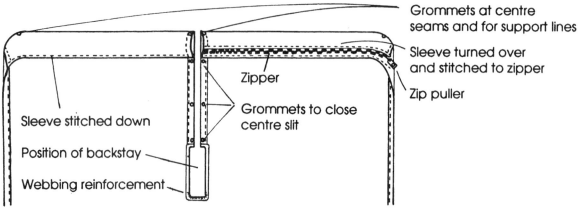

Grommets at centre seams and for support lines

Sleeve turned over and stitched to zipper

Zip puller

Zipper

Grommets to close centre slit

Sleeve stitched down

Position of backstay

Webbing reinforcement

**Fig 55**

## The Bimini Sock

When you wish to leave the bimini closed, with the frame folded back, but do not want the effort of removing the canvas or the whole frame, it is worth making an easily fitted cover. This will look better than a straightforward lashing round the cloth and frames – and more importantly, it will prevent dust or rain collecting in the folds, as well as protecting the stitching from the sun.

For the dimensions, fold the frame back and roll the canvas round it. Measure the cover from one side to the other, adding 10cm at each end. Then measure around it at the fattest part and add 10cm for turn-overs. If the bimini is split to allow it to go aft of the backstay, mark this point, which should be at the centre.

If you have offcuts of the same material as the top itself, they can be stitched together to make a long rectangle for the sleeve. Turn under both long edges by 1cm and sew them down, then turn in each short end by 5cm and sew along the inner edge only to form a hem for the draw-strings.

If both frames are forward of the backstay, pin, tack or stick one side of an open-ended zipper to the inside of the lower edge of the sleeve, leaving the teeth showing on the outside, and lining up the opening end with the hem stitching. Sew it in place, reinforcing the ends. For the other half of the zipper, draw a line 5cm in from the upper inside edge of the sleeve as a guide-line and lay the zip, teeth facing upwards, to this, ensuring that both sides will match. (Fig 56)

Run a length of 3mm cord through each hem (tacking it in place in the centre) to pull the cover tight around the frame at each end after the zip is fastened. If the cover will rest against the back-stay, it may be advisable to position a reinforce-ment patch onto it at that point.

If the back of the frame is aft of the backstay, two open-ended zippers will be required and also a split in the cover at the centre. The simplest way to make this is to make a join in the fabric at this point and stitch the two sections together for only a quarter of the join, starting about 10–15cm up from the lower edge. By doing this , the zipper overlap at the upper edge will keep the elements away from the other half of the fastener. It will be necessary to reinforce the ends of the join before turning the edges to the inside. (Fig 57)

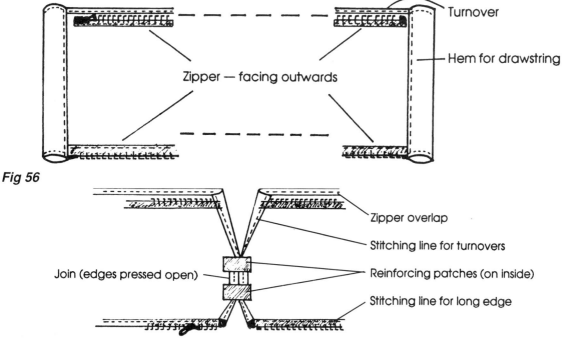

Turnover

Hem for drawstring

Zipper — facing outwards

**Fig 56**

Zipper overlap

Stitching line for turnovers

Join (edges pressed open)

Reinforcing patches (on inside)

Stitching line for long edge

**Fig 57**

If using a single strip of cloth, a reinforced cut out will be needed. The easiest way to make this is to cut it out just inside the turn-over line, clip the corners so that the fold will lie flat and then strengthen it with a folded strip of 2cm wide nylon webbing stitched around. (Fig 58)

With either method, insert the zippers as described before, but be sure that the 'pullers' are at the outer end when closed, as they are stronger than the 'slot-in' ends.

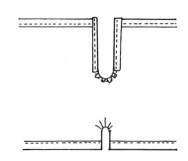

**Fig 58**

# Spray Dodgers and Fender Stowage

*What you will need*

## Spray Dodgers
UV and water-resistant (or waterproof) material
3–4mm cord
No 1 grommets
Saddle-eyes

## Fender Pockets
Material as above
Shock-cord
Tailor's chalk, pins, straight-edge, square (or weighted line), thread, scissors etc.

*Spray dodgers running along the side of the cockpit give protection at sea and privacy in marinas.*

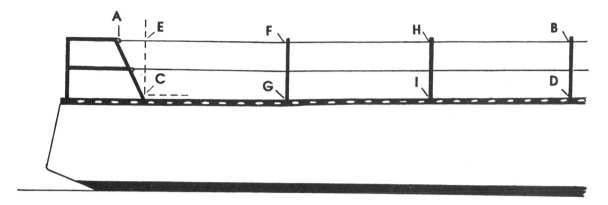

**Fig 59**

Any boat that finds itself in a crowded harbour or marina will need fenders – the bigger the better. But unless you have a large cockpit locker that is kept free for fender stowage (not many boats have that extravagance) there will always be a problem of where to keep them when at sea or in a deserted anchorage where they are not required. If they are left tied along the side-deck they become yet another hazard to trip over and if they are left exposed to the sun they soon become sticky and unpleasant to handle and will also perish faster. Stowing them below occupies valuable accommodation space and even worse, if they happen to be under a bunk, you cannot reach them quickly if needed in an emergency.

The answer is simple – fender pockets. These can be made to hold almost any size of fender and can be independent of, or added to spray cloths.

## Here are some ideas.

If you do not already have spray cloths, or dodgers as they are often known, they are simple to make and will offer protection from the worst of wind and water and a certain increased privacy in the cockpit when moored. These need to be fitted first and the fender pockets added later.

## 1 Centre Cockpits

If your boat has a centre cockpit you may not wish to enclose the entire stern area. In this case the spray cloths need only to run from the front of the pushpit to the stanchion nearest the front of the cockpit. Following Fig 59, measure from A (front of the pushpit) to B (back of stanchion) along the lifeline, and then from C to D along the top of the toe-rail. With a square (or weighted cord) find the right-angle at C. The point where this touches the top lifeline we shall call E. Take the length from A to E. Measure the height E–C, F–G, H–I and B–D. If there is more than 2cm difference in these, you will also need to measure E–F, F–H and H–B. (If the stanchion at B–D is not at right angles to the toe-rail you will have to adjust the top or bottom length as at C.)

Your drawing should now look similar to Fig 60

Check that both port and starboard side measurements are the same (within 1cm) If not, make a second drawing, taking care to label which side it is!

To determine how much material will be required, you should add the hem allowances. Spray cloths should be stretched tight, so if you add 3cm on all sides but turn over 5cm in total on each edge, the finished cloth will be smaller than your drawing indicates, but will make a good fit when fastened into position.

When you have measured one cloth with its hem allowance, you can determine if it is possible to cut both port and starboard sides from a single width of fabric – a considerable saving. If the combined height of the two cloths is marginally greater than the width of the material, trim a centimetre or two from the top edges of each, rather than from the bottom. Cut out the two panels and mark a line round each, 2cm in from the edge, (on the right side of the cloth) for

47

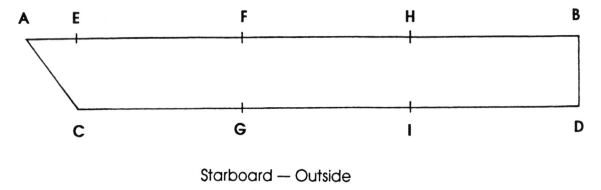

Starboard — Outside

**Fig 60**

the first fold line, then another line 3cm in from the first, for the second fold. Crease the first one over to the wrong side all round, then the second and stitch round the inner and outer edges of the hem (preferably with zig-zag).

The strongest method of fastening spray cloths to the lifeline and stanchions is by lashing them with 3mm or 4mm cord through No 1 grommets in the hem. These should be set into each corner and about 15cm apart along the length and about 10cm apart along the short sides. If the boat has an extruded toe-rail with holes as in Fig 59, use them to tie the lower edge down. If not, one could rivet a small saddle-eye to the stanchions at points C, G, I and D as attachment points for the lower edge. (In this case do not insert the grommets in to the lower edge until you have fitted the spray cloth, so that you can mark their positions accurately.) If the cloth is only stretched between the pushpit and the first stanchion, a screw-eye

or a saddle-eye should be fitted at each third of the distance between them, as well as at point C and the base of the stanchion.

Having checked the fit of your spray cloth, lay it down flat with the outside facing you. Decide where you wish to place the fender pockets – the best place is at the aft end of the cloth. Say, for example, you wish to carry three on each side; pick the three most similar in size, lay them on the cloth next to each other 5cm from the end and with a space of 5cm between each one. Measure from the edge, over the first one (quite loosely) to the first space, then over the remaining two in the same manner. This will give you the length of material (add 5cm for turnovers at each end) for the pocket. Now measure the height of the right-angles to the top and bottom of the cloth. Mark with tailor's chalk a line on the outside of and between each fender as a stitching guide. (Fig 61)

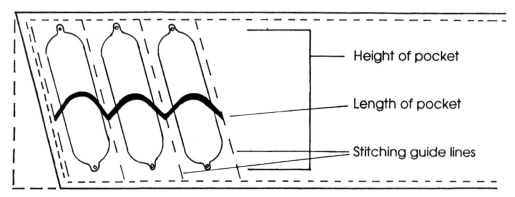

Height of pocket

Length of pocket

Stitching guide lines

**Fig 61**

48

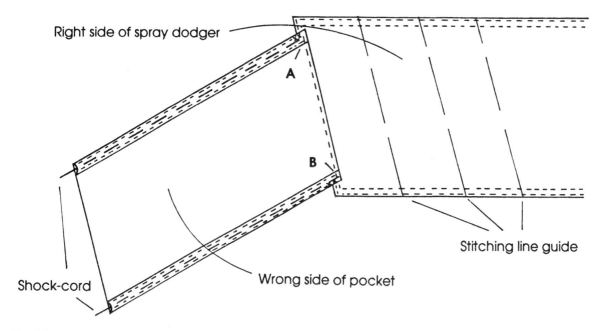

Right side of spray dodger

A

B

Stitching line guide

Shock-cord

Wrong side of pocket

**Fig 62**

The easiest way to cut the pocket at the correct angle is to mark a line 5cm down from the selvedge at the top of the cloth and parallel to it, the length to be 5cm longer than the finished pocket. Lay the spray cloth onto the material with the top edge to the line and mark along the angled end. Take it off and measure from the top line for the fold; 5cm below this is the cutting line.

Cut the forward short edge of the pocket parallel to the aft edge, turn over the hems at top and bottom and stitch along them at the inner and outer edge , leaving a space of 3cm between the sewing lines. Lay the aft edge of the pocket 1cm inside the stitching line closest to the angled side of the spray cloth (right sides together). Mark the sewing line and machine along it. (Fig 62)

Unpick the stitches at A and B and thread a length of 4mm shock-cord along each hem; sew through the cord and the cloth at this point to hold it in place and re-stitch the unpicked thread, leaving the free end of the shock-cord emerging from the other end of the pocket.

Lay the fenders into place and fold the pocket over them with the edges parallel to the edges of the spray cloth. Tuck the pocket down between the first and second fender (making sure that the spray cloth remains stretched out and flat) and put a couple of pins top and bottom to hold it in place. Do the same with the second and third fenders and at the end turn under any excess cloth, leaving sufficient to run a line of stitching down the turned-over edge. With a ruler or straight-edge, draw chalk lines on the pocket to match the stitching guide lines, then sew along them. Because of the shock-cord you must reinforce the ends of the stitching lines just into the top and bottom hems. (Fig 63)

Now pull the lower shock-cord tight enough so that the bottom of each pocket is gathered flat against the spray cloth. Oversew by hand at the points D, E and F through the shock-cord, the hem of the material and the backing cloth. (Use a darning needle and a strong thread or dental floss.) Follow the same method at the top at A, B and C, but leave the shock-cord a little looser to enable the fenders to be removed easily. Make sure that the forward end of the shock-cord is securely sewn in place, and trim off the surplus.

Now fasten the spray cloth in position, with a thin line at each corner to hold it on. Start lacing it in place from one corner. (ie. from the base of the pushpit, working upwards and along the lifeline.) The best cord for the lacing is 3mm or

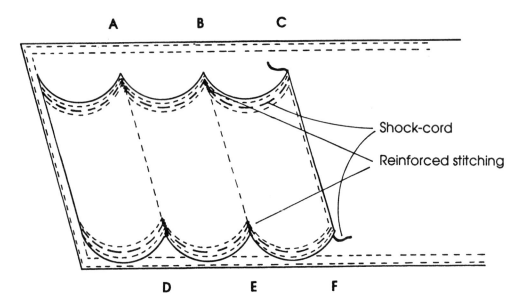

A    B    C

Shock-cord

Reinforced stitching

D    E    F

**Fig 63**

4mm braided leech-line or a similar soft cord. (If you use saddle-eyes or screw-eyes at the toe-rail, tie the lower edge down with separate short lengths of line.)

Put the fenders into the pockets with the tie at the top; fasten them with a clove-hitch or slip knot to the lifeline – and that's it. They are easy to get at, protected from the sun, cannot get lost and are out of your way. (Fig 64)

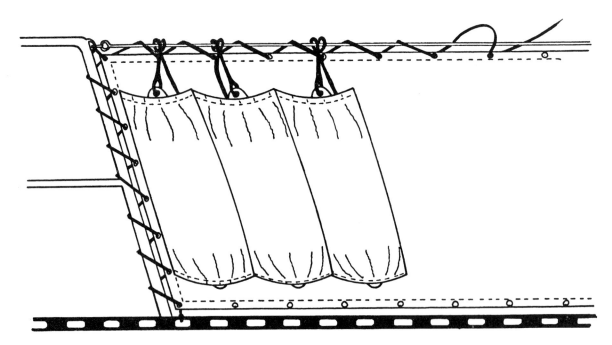

**Fig 64**

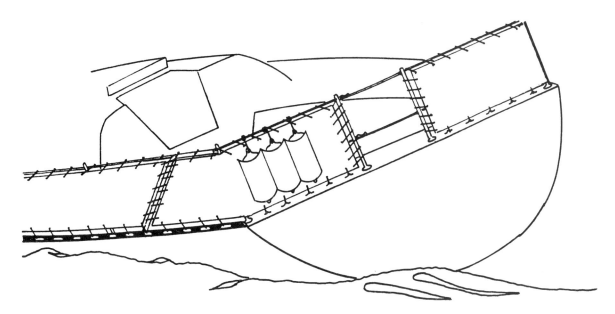

**Fig 65**

## 2 Aft Cockpits

If your boat has an aft cockpit and you want to be protected from following winds and spray, it is better to make a separate dodger (spray cloth) for the stern. If the pushpit has a stern-gate, this should be left unobstructed and the cloths run from either side to a position just aft at the angled stanchion at the front of the pushpit. (Fig 65)

Provided that the corner stanchion is at right-angles to the deck, the measurements can be taken as before. If not, cut the cloth oversize, tack it to the railing at each end and at the curve, and mark it with chalk from the inside just below the railing. Transfer these lines to the outside where they will become the fold line for the finished size of the spray cloth. Also mark the position of the corner pushpit stanchion, as if you want to fit the fender pockets on the stern-rail they should not extend beyond this point.

Once you have made stern spray cloths, you can decide how many fenders you can fit on each side. Then make the pockets as before, but taking the shape of the dodger on the stern. (Fig 66)

Position of corner stanchion

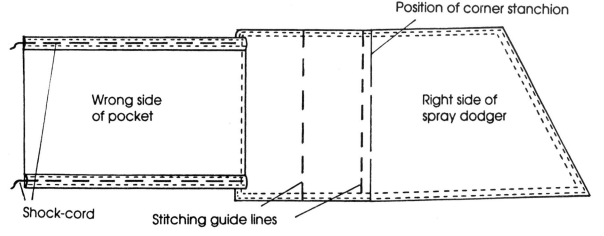

Wrong side of pocket

Right side of spray dodger

Shock-cord

Stitching guide lines

**Fig 66**

If you do not have a stern-gate, you can run the spray cloth all round to the angled stanchion on each side, using the entire stern area for fender pockets.

## Fender Pocket Size and Shape

The size of the pockets will vary depending on the size of the fenders. For a neater looking job (if your fenders are different sizes) make the pockets to fit the largest.

If you use (as many yachts do) canvas-covered tyres for fenders, they also can be stored in outboard pockets. To make these, lay out the material and draw round the tyre, carrying the side lines up to form a U-shape with the top of the U 5cm above the top of the tyre. This will be the front of the pocket. The cutting line should be 2cm outside the first line. (Fig 67)

Cut a strip 2.5cm wider than the tyre across the tread and long enough to go all the way around the pocket at the top edges. Turn one long side of the strip over 1cm and stitch it down.

Matching one end of the strip to the top of the U-shaped pocket front (right sides together), stitch it round the front, 1cm in from the cutting line. (Fig 68)

Insert a grommet at X as a drain-hole. Turn over 3cm at the top and sides and stitch along the inner edge only. Run a length of shock-cord through and seize it 1cm back from the turn-over. Leaving the other end free for the moment, place the pocket, inside-out as it looks in Fig 68, on to the spray cloth in the desired position and draw round it. This line marks the stitching line for the sides of the pocket. Pin the pocket to the cloth and sew round it (Fig 69) leaving unstitched the last 5cm from the top on the other side where the shock-cord is not fastened. With the spray cloth held flat, put the tyre into the pocket and draw up the shock-cord till it gathers over the edge of the tyre. Seize it to the hem 5cm in from the edge, cut off the surplus and pin and sew the last 5cm into place.

As before, use the fender line to tie to the pushpit or lifeline.

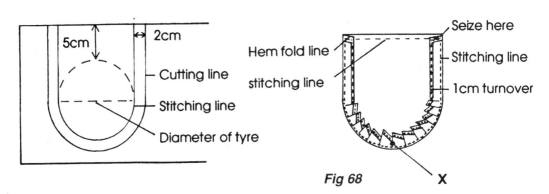

**Fig 67**

**Fig 68**

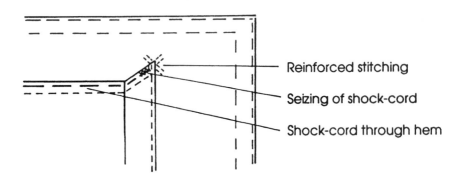

**Fig 69**

# Sheet Pockets

*What you will need*

Material as for spray dodgers
Shock-cord
Velcro
3mm cord

*A sensible place to stow the headsail sheets when moored. They remain out-of-the way and can dry out at their leisure if sodden on arrival.*

Rather than leaving sheets coiled on deck or tied to the lifeline when in port, where they can attract dirt and are subjected to the sun's attention, why not add to the inside of your spray cloths special pockets to contain them? These can also be useful when sailing, as holders for binoculars, torches or a drop of the hard stuff.

If the dodgers are fastened inside the lower lifeline (as in the photo), the pocket can extend the full depth of the cloth, leaving sufficient room for the fastening grommets at top and bottom. If the dodgers are attached outside, the pockets will have to be longer and shallower to fit between the top and lower lifeline.

In either case, cut the pocket 20% wider at the top than the bottom, adding 1cm turnover at the sides and lower edge, and 3cm at the top for the hem. (Fig 70)

Turn over 1cm at each side and the lower edge, and press down. Then fold over 3cm on the upper edge and zig-zag stitch it down along the cutting line. Run a length of shock-cord through the hem and stitch it in at one end 1cm in from the edge turnover. (Fig 71)

Draw up the cord till the gathered top edge is slightly shorter than the lower edge, stitch the shock-cord through the hem, 1cm in, and cut of the excess.

Measure the lower edge and sides, mark on the inside of the dodger your guide-lines, with the sides at right-angles to the lower edge. Pin or tack the pocket in place and zig-zag stitch it on, reinforcing the upper corners. The cloth will pucker at the top edge of the pocket, but when lashed on, will lie flat as the shock-cord is stretched. This will give the tension to hold the pocket contents securely.

To make the pocket more spray-proof, cut a flap to the same length as the lower edge and one third of the pocket height, turn over 1cm on one length on both sides and stitch down. Turn the other long edge over 3cm and stitch a strip of Velcro on the inside of the hem at the edge. Mark the centre of the flap on the outside with chalk.

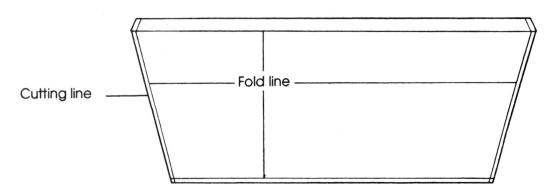

Cutting line — Fold line —

**Fig 70**

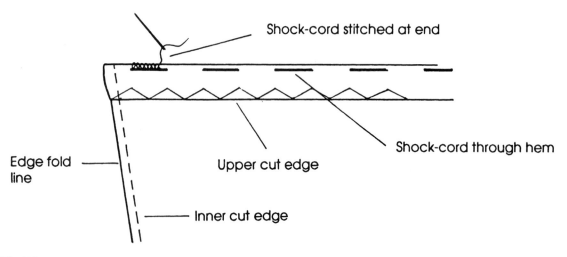

Shock-cord stitched at end

Edge fold line

Upper cut edge

Shock-cord through hem

Inner cut edge

**Fig 71**

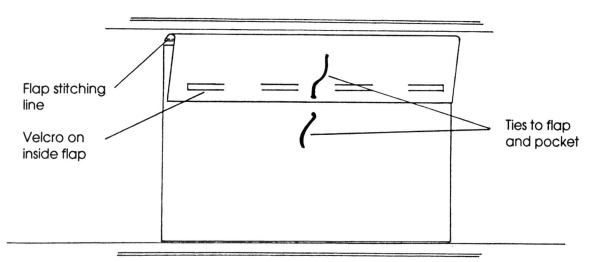

Flap stitching line

Velcro on inside flap

Ties to flap and pocket

**Fig 72**

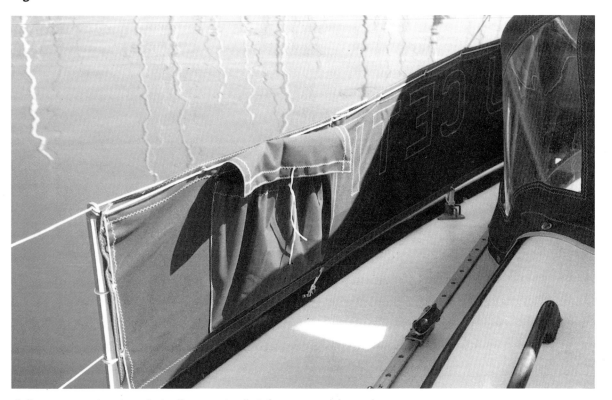

*A flap over a sheet pocket offers protection from sun, rain and spray.*

Lay the flap over the pocket body, Velcro side down, with the top edge just above, but matching the pocket sides. Zig-zag along the upper edge, reinforcing both ends. Mark the pocket centre at the lower flap hem (allowing the flap to fold over loosely), and at each end. With these marks as a guide-line, stitch the other half of the Velcro to the pocket, matching the centres. If necessary, sew a short length of 2mm cord to the pocket and another to the flap as additional security ties. (Fig 72)

Another, possibly stronger, method of making longer and shallower pockets is to make them in one piece complete with the flap-over, and then stitch them to the dodgers – or to make them so that they can be attached separately to the life-lines.

Following Fig 62, cut the pocket fabric, allowing 3cm extra at the top and bottom for hems and 1cm at each side. Turn the sides in by this amount (you may have to clip at fold B so that the turnover lies flat), then turn over the hems at top

and bottom and stitch them down.(Fig 73)

Sew a strip of Velcro along the top hem, on the inside. Fold the pocket at B and then at A, and mark the position for the other half of the strip. (It should be 2cm up from the line of the top hem edge.) Mark the position of the centre rectangle (the pocket back) onto the spray cloth and pin it in place. Stitch as in Fig 74.

Fold at B, matching the sides, and stitch up to fold A and back again, reinforcing each end. (Fig 75)

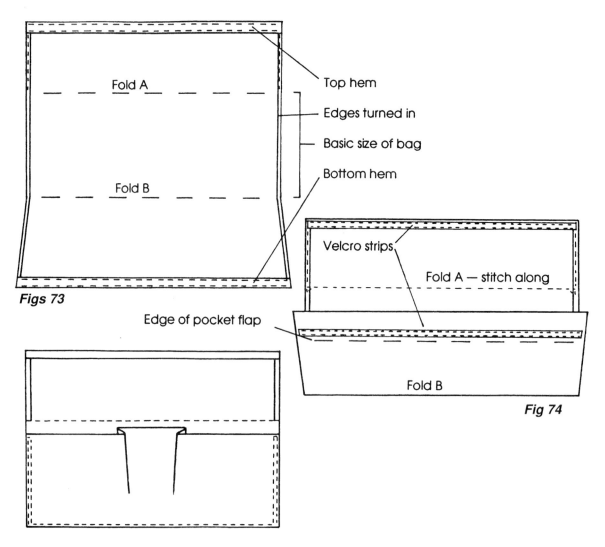

Fold A

Top hem

Edges turned in

Basic size of bag

Bottom hem

Fold B

**Figs 73**

Velcro strips

Fold A — stitch along

Edge of pocket flap

Fold B

**Fig 74**

**Fig 75**

56

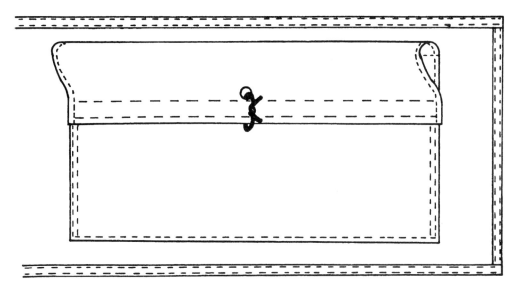

**Fig 76**

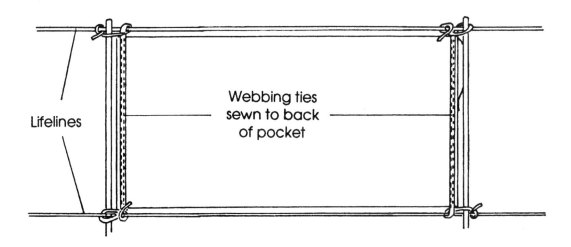

**Fig 77**

The Velcro should be strong enough to hold the pocket closed, but for additional security, put a grommet in the centre of the flap, just above the Velcro, and stitch a length of 3mm leech-line to the pocket front. Thread one end through the grommet and tie the ends together. (Fig 76)

If you wish the sheet pockets to be independent of the dodger, they can be made in the same way and fastened to the lifelines by webbing strips stitched to the back of the pocket from fold A to fold B at each side and tied on as in Fig 77.

Another method of fastening these pockets is by inserting grommets at equal spacing just below fold A and just above fold B, and using these to run a line through and round the upper and lower lifelines.

# Fender Nets

*What you will need*

Netting
2mm cord
3mm cord
Shock-cord

*Nets provide safe and convenient stowage for varying shapes of fender.*

If your boat already has safety netting around the lifelines, fenders can also be stowed in net pockets on either the inside or the outside of the netting. Cut another piece to the same height and to the required length. Lash it onto the lower edge and up each side, and run a line of shock-cord in and out of the top edge. Tie off one end and stretch the shock-cord slightly to tension it and to hold the fenders securely and then tie off the remaining end.

It is also possible to make fender pockets from netting to fit between two stanchions. Take the measurement between two stanchions, and either fold the netting in half lengthwise, or take a piece twice the length and fold it half down the width. If the netting is wide enough when laid flat, to be twice the length of the stanchion, fold it in half lengthwise and lash each side together with 2mm cord. (Fig 78)

Run a length of shock-cord through one long edge, and a length of 3mm line through the other, and also through the fold. (Fig 79)

Leave enough cord at the top and bottom to lash each side (half-way up from the bottom and down from the top) around the stanchion and top lifeline.

If the netting is not wide enough, take double the length between the stanchions, fold it across the width and sew it together along the lower edge and up the open side, and fasten as before. (Fig 80)

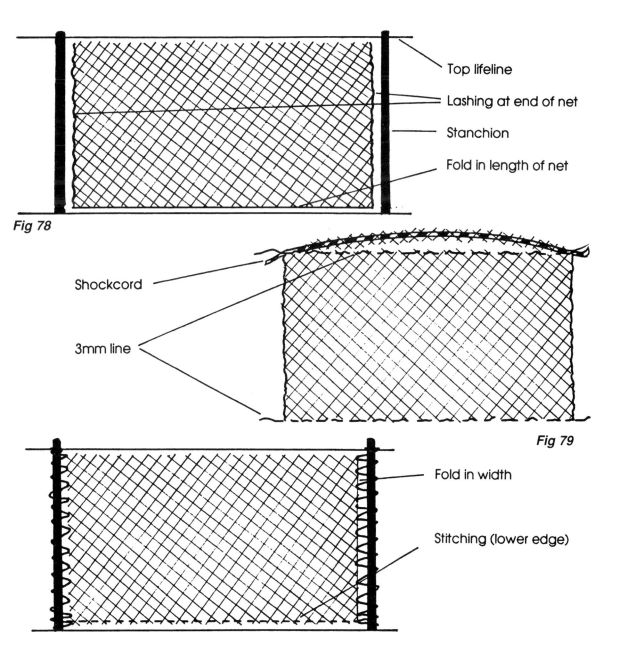

Top lifeline

Lashing at end of net

Stanchion

Fold in length of net

*Fig 78*

Shockcord

3mm line

*Fig 79*

Fold in width

Stitching (lower edge)

*Fig 80*

# Home-made Fenders and Fender Pads

*What you will need*

Cushion foam
Rope
Clear plastic sheeting
Masking Tape
Strong Canvas (for the cover)

*An attractive, strong and inexpensive fender*

Fenders are an expensive necessity on any boat, especially in a marina, where your yacht is liable to damage – or be damaged by – your neighbours or the jetty if left unprotected. During winter storms, it is disheartening to see your expensive fenders becoming punctured and deflated, not to mention the damage caused to the hull. It is simple to make your own semi-solid fenders for little or no cost.

In most marinas, especially over the winter season, there will be boats renewing bunk or saloon cushions and throwing the old ones away. Here is a good source for the foam which you will require. Its condition is immaterial, but the thicker it is, the better. The ideal size is 2m or more long, 75–100cm wide and 8–15cm thick.

Saloon cushions are likely to be near enough rectangular, but if you find old shaped bunk cushions, wider at one end than the other, they are also ideal provided that you can trim off any angles and cut both sides roughly the same. (See Figure 81)

All you need is the foam, a length of line (an old mooring warp or sheet etc) five times the length of the widest part of the foam, a sheet of clear plastic about 80cm wider and longer than the cushion, insulating tape and some cheap material to make the cover.

Double the line and tie an overhand knot at the centre to form the eye. If the foam is a rectangle lay the line across the width at one end. (See Figure 82)

If you are using bunk cushion foam, lay the line on the narrowest end, with the knot level with the wider end. (See Figure 83)

Roll the foam tightly round the rope into a sausage shape and tape it round both ends and in the centre to hold it firmly. Take the free ends of rope, tie them together where they emerge from the roll, bring the ends up either side and pass them under the eye in the opposite direction. (See Figure 84)

Tie the two ends together with a reef knot and tuck the remaining rope back into the centre.

Lay the foam sausage onto one end of the plastic sheet, equidistant from each side and roll it up as tightly as possible, fastening it with tape

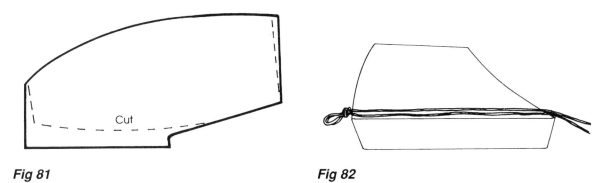

**Fig 81**

**Fig 82**

*As things should look at the stage illustrated in Fig 82*

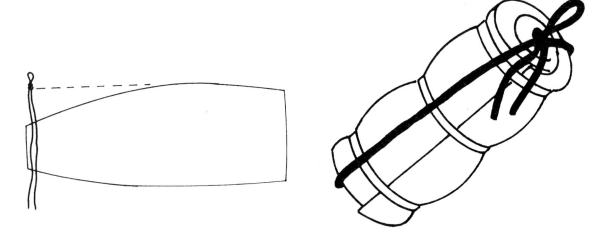

**Fig 83**

**Fig 84**

*The fender at the stage shown in Fig 84*

*Now it begins to look like a fender.*

just above and below the inner tape at both ends and around the centre.

At the top of the fender, gather the plastic together just below the knot and fasten it with waxed thread in a tight double clove-hitch to prevent rain soaking the foam.

At the bottom, fold it as if you were wrapping a

bottle and add several turns of tape to keep it secure. Make a few holes in the plastic at the bottom. Although this means that the foam can absorb water, they will enable it to drain faster.

Directions for the fender cover follow on page 64.

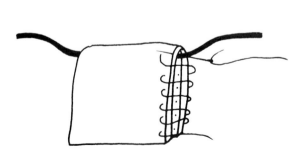

**Fig 85**

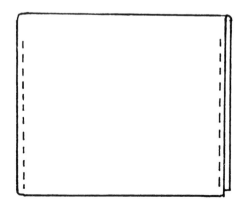

**Fig 86**

## Fender Pads

Using old foam or discarded boat cushions, cut a rectangle twice the length of the width. Fold the cushion in half, run a rope through the fold and roughly stitch the two side edges together through the foam, catching the rope in the stitching at the upper corners. (See Figure 85)

If you have any old canvas or sailcloth, it is better to cover these simple folded foam-cushion pads as they will then last longer and provide better protection for the hull.

Take a piece of cloth the width plus 2cm, and double the depth plus 4cm of the pad. Stitch down each side, leaving 2cm unsewn at the fold on each side. (See Figure 86)

Turn the cloth the other way out, slip it over the pad and feed the ropes at the corners through the corresponding openings at the top corners of the cover. Loosely stitch the lower edges together.

Tie the pad to the jetty, *not* to the boat, thus ensuring that however much the boat moves, the hull is protected from damage.

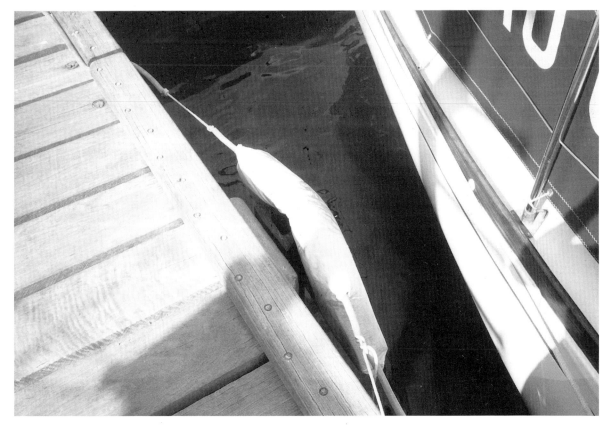

*Fender pads are useful for emergencies as they are quick to make, but they are also a sensible idea when moored at a berth for any lengthy period.*

# Fender Covers

*What you will need*

Old sailcloth, canvas, Acrylic, stretch towelling or any other cloth that is in reasonable condition.
No1 grommets
Shock-cord or thin line.

*A cover on a hand-made fender on the left and on a production fender on the right.*

To lengthen the life of your fenders and preserve the condition of your topsides, removable and washable fender covers are worth considering. These do not have to be made from expensive material as they will get damaged sooner or later. It is a lot cheaper to make another cover than to buy a new fender.

The covers need to be easy to remove and rinse out as they can trap salt, dust and grit which will abrade the hull.

**Material to use.**

*Old sailcloth*
Unless this is very lightweight or worn and supple (in which case it is likely to tear easily), it will be stiff and awkward to work with, especially when it comes to tensioning the drawstring at each end. Better keep spare sailcloth for patching the sails.

*Canvas*
If it is strong and heavy enough to last, it can present the same problems as sailcloth.

*Acrylic*
This is an expensive material – too good to use for this purpose and no better than cheaper alternatives.

*Stretch towelling*
Available from most general fabric stores and it is often possible to find 'roll-ends' or remnants for less than half-price.

*Knitted stretch cotton jersey (T-shirt material)*
This can sometimes be found in tubular form on rolls. This has the advantage that it can be stretched to fit any size of fender, but the disadvantage of being fairly thin and difficult to machine sew.

For standard shaped oblong fenders, measure from the top of the eye to the bottom of the fender and then around the circumference. Cut a rectangle of material this size plus 2cm on the circumference as a seam allowance. Stitch this side up, leaving a small gap at the top and bottom of the seam. (See Figure 87) Turn over a hem at the top and bottom edges with a drawstring emerging through the gap in the seam. Pull tight and thread it through the eye at each end or tie the ends together.

*Other ideas*
If, like many cruising yachts, you are trying to save money and live on a tight budget and wish to protect your fenders, do not discard any of the following.

*Worn-out jogging (or stretch) pants.*
For small fenders, cut off below the knee, use the lower hem for one drawstring and turn over the upper edge for the top hem. For larger fenders use the thigh part of the pants, turning over top and bottom edges for the drawstring.

*Cut-off Jeans*
When the knees are worn through, and you turn them into shorts, save the legs. If your fenders are too fat to fit into the legs, split each leg down the inner seam and join them together (to fit the fender's circumference). Turn over the upper hem and cut off the lower edge to the right length, allowing for the turn-over.

*Old T-shirts*
If they have a design, turn them inside-out. Mark the stitching line on the outside, from the neck (which will take the upper drawstring). (See Figure 88)

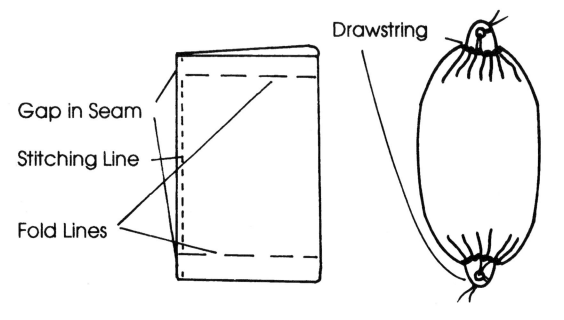

Drawstring

Gap in Seam

Stitching Line

Fold Lines

**Fig 87**

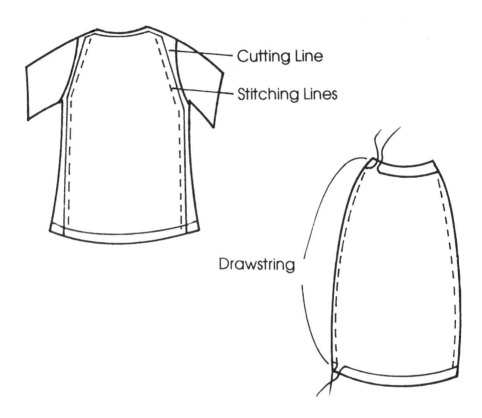

**Fig 88**

If you use old car tyres as fenders, they must be covered, as the marks they will leave on your topsides will take much scrubbing to remove, not to mention the comments you'll get from the boat next to you.

Tyre covers should be made from the thickest canvas (or sailcloth). Refer to Figs 67 & 68 for the pattern.

You will need to cut two U-shaped pieces for the front and back, and instead of turning the side strip over 1cm, join it to the second U-shape. Instead of a single grommet at X, put two, one either side which will enable you to mark on the tyre where to cut the holes for the rope. The hem will come at the bottom of the tyre and can be gathered with shock-cord or thin rope. (Fig 89)

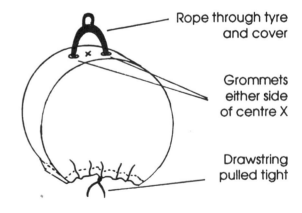

**Fig 89**

# Horseshoe Buoy and Life-ring Holders

*What you will need*

Material to match dodgers
2cm wide webbing
Shock-cord
Velcro
No 1 grommet

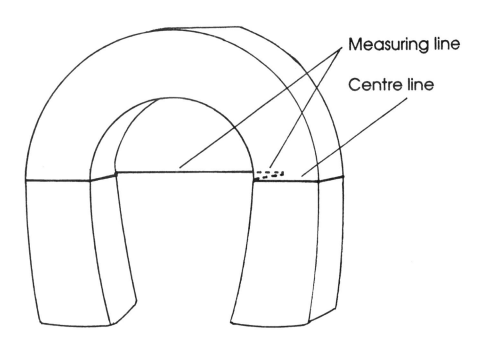

Measuring line

Centre line

***Fig 90***

These can be awkward items to stow, but they need to be within reach and easy to throw at all times. If your boat does not have a bracket to hold them, it is possible to make a holder out of fabric, either sewn on to the dodger or separate to be attached to the lifelines or pushpit.

## Horseshoe Buoys

If the holder is to be attached to a dodger, then this should be made first as already described. Consider the position of the horseshoe, remembering that it should be within easy reach of the helmsman at all times. Obviously it is better to carry two, so that on whichever tack the helmsman is sailing one can be quite close, but if only one is to be carried consider its location carefully. Mark the final position on the appropriate dodger with chalk.

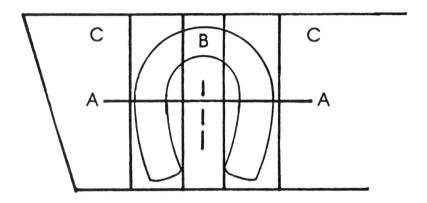

**Fig 91**

Place the horseshoe on a flat surface and mark the centre (from top to bottom). Now measure from the outside of the horseshoe (on the floor), up and over one arm of the shoe and then along the floor again (passing the centre) to the other arm which is again measured up, across and back down to the floor.(Fig 90)

Add 4cm to this measurement and cut a strip of cloth that long and 15cm wide. Turn over 1cm hem all round and stitch it down.

Place the horseshoe in the required position on the outside of the dodger and draw the outline in chalk, marking also the top to bottom centre line – A. Draw a line from each of the inner bottom corners of the horseshoe to the top of the cloth at right-angles – B, and then another vertical at the outermost edge of the outside line – C. The result should resemble Fig 91.

Mark the centre (top to bottom) between lines B where they are crossed by A. Match the centre of the holding strip to this mark with the top hem (facing inwards) lying along line A. Pin either side of the centre with the strip opened out and draw chalk lines over the strip to follow lines B. Sew round this rectangle, reinforcing the stitching at each corner. Pin the two short edges of the strip along lines C, starting from the top at corners A–C and stitch them firmly in place. This will give you the loops to hold both arms of the horseshoe. To support the top, take a piece of webbing 2cm wide and 10cm long, fold it in half and stitch it (with the loop facing down) at the top centre of the inner outline. (Fig 92)

If the buoy has a strobe light attached, then this will be better stowed inside the dodger to protect it from the elements. To make a pocket for this, turn the dodger over and place the light, bulb facing downwards, over the stitching that marks the rectangle in the centre of the horseshoe. Measure from one side over the fattest part of the light to the other, Lines B to B, and add 3cm.

Cut a rectangle of cloth this length and 26mm wide, turn in the hem of 1cm each end and sew it down. At the top and bottom turn over 3cm and stitch the inner edge only.

On the inside of the spray cloth, pin the strip at each end to lines B (the top edge should extend 5cm above line A) and sew them down, running the stitching 5cm towards the centre on the lower hem.

Unpick a couple of stitches at each end of the top and bottom hem and run a length of shock-cord through; cross-stitch it by hand at one end and re-stitch the unpicked thread. Pull the free end of the cord at the bottom until the hem is gathered flat against the cloth. Now cross-stitch at and cut off the excess and re-sew the unpicked thread. (Fig 93)

Place the light in the pocket and take up on the top shock-cord until it is held in place but can be extracted easily. Catch the end through the hem and redo the stitching. To hold the upper part of the light, cut a strip of 2cm wide webbing 25cm long (heat-sealed at the ends), sew onto one end of this a 5cm long piece of Velcro. At the other end (and 2cm in from it, on the reverse side) stitch the matching 5cm. With the light in place (the bulb should stick out from the bottom of the

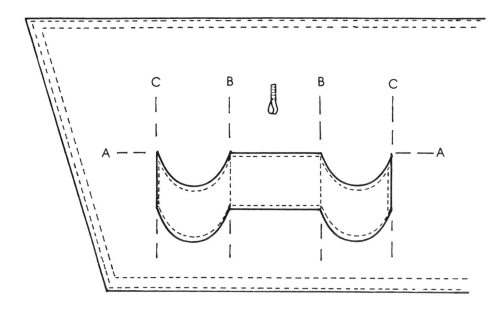

**Fig 92**

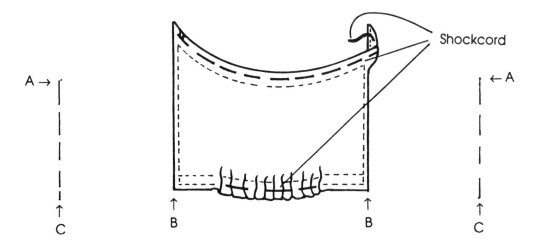

**Fig 93**

pocket), pin the centre of the webbing to the dodger cloth so that the fastened Velcro will hold the top end of the light in place and the 2cm of spare webbing at the end will form a tag to pull it open. Stitch the webbing firmly to the dodger cloth at the centre. (Fig 94)

The line attaching the strobe light to the horseshoe buoy can be stowed in the light pocket, carefully coiled so that it will not become tangled when thrown.

To ensure that the horseshoe buoy will stay in place in bad weather and yet can be easily released, run a length of shock-cord through the webbing loop, and with both ends together, bring them outside the horseshoe; attach them to one hook to catch on the lifeline. This method enables you to free the buoy without losing the shock-cord fastener, and without moving from the cockpit. (Fig 95)

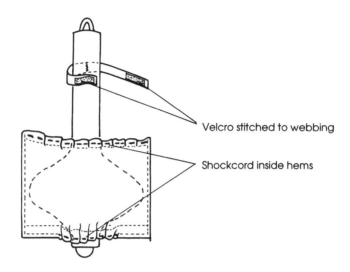

**Fig 94**

Velcro stitched to webbing

Shockcord inside hems

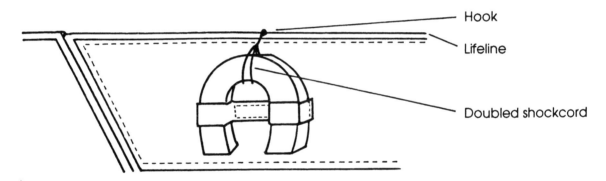

**Fig 95**

Hook

Lifeline

Doubled shockcord

## Life-rings

The easiest way to stow these on the outside of the dodgers is to make U-shaped pockets for them to sit in.

To find the size, lay the ring onto a piece of cloth and draw round it with chalk. Measure the diameter and draw it on. Mark 10cm up and draw another line the same length. Extend the sides up to this to form a shallow U-shape. Cut out 2cm outside the U and along the upper line. (Fig 96)

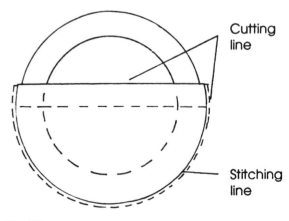

Cutting line

Stitching line

**Fig 96**

Lay this in position on the outside of the dodger and draw round it, stopping 5cm down from the top line at each side.

Measure the thickness of the ring and add 2cm. Cut a strip this wide and long enough to go round the outside of the U. Turn under 1cm on one long edge and sew it down. Stitch the other long edge to the outside of the U, notching the seam allowance when you come to the curve. Fold over 5cm along the top of the U and both ends of the strip and stitch along twice. Press the seam allowances towards the strip and stitch it down. (Fig 97)

Put a grommet in the centre of the strip at the bottom as a drain hole.

Match the turned-over edge of the strip to the U-shape on the outside of the spray cloth, pin it in place and sew it on, reinforcing the top corners with two or three rows of stitching. As with the horseshoe buoy, attach a loop of webbing at the top to hold the shock-cord and hook. Inside the

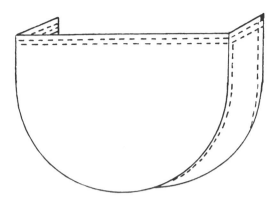

*Fig 97*

centre front, to hold the ring in the pocket, sew a 5cm strip of Velcro, put the ring into place and mark where the Velcro touches the spray cloth, then sew the matching 5cm of Velcro onto it. (Fig 98)

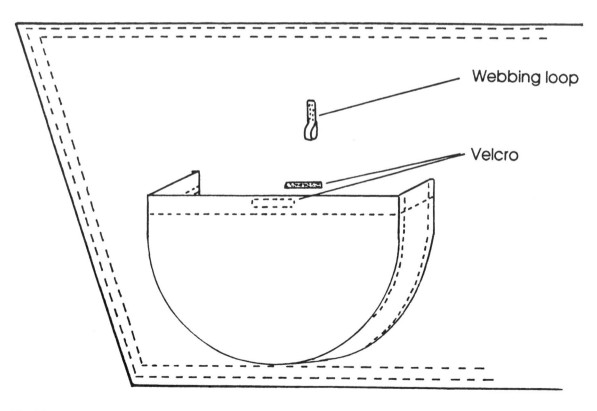

Webbing loop

Velcro

*Fig 98*

## Alternative Life-saving Fitments

A cheaper and simpler method of fastening a horseshoe buoy or a life-ring to the lifelines if you do not have dodgers, uses only two lengths of shock-cord, three or four hooks and a sheet bag fastened to the lifelines.

Use the stanchion most convenient to the cockpit (or to the helming position). Take a length of unstretched shock-cord (5mm–6mm) the width of the horseshoe, and fasten it at the centre to the stanchion with a clove hitch, just below the bottom lifeline. Slide a hook onto each end, but do not tie them off until you are sure of the length. For the vertical fastening, measure between the upper and lower lifelines, and cut a length of unstretched shock-cord to this measurement. Tie or stitch one end securely round the stanchion just below the clove hitch, and thread a hook onto the other end, again not making it fast until the tension is adjusted.

Lay the horseshoe outside the lifelines, centre the top to the stanchion close to the upper lifeline, and tie it loosely in position. Pass each free end round the 'leg', hook onto the lower lifeline and draw up the cord until it is holding the horseshoe firmly against the stanchion; make off the hook at this point. (This can be done either by putting a strong overhand knot at the end or by stitching the cord itself through the hook.)

For the vertical attachment, run the shock-cord outside the horseshoe and hook onto the upper lifeline, then tension the cord and make it off. (Fig 99)

For a life-ring, fasten it the same way horizontally, and use an equal length of shock-cord (attached at the centre of the lower lifeline on each side of the stanchion) to allow one end to hook to the base of the stanchion, and the other to the upper lifeline. (Fig 100)

To hold the floating line attached to the horseshoe or ring, make a sheet bag as already described, with, if necessary, an additional insert pocket to hold the strobe light. The line pocket should be tied to the lifelines, facing inwards with the line lead under the lower lifeline before being made off to the ring or horseshoe. If a 'dan-buoy' is also attached make sure that its line will run freely when the horseshoe is unhooked and thrown over the side. (Fig 101)

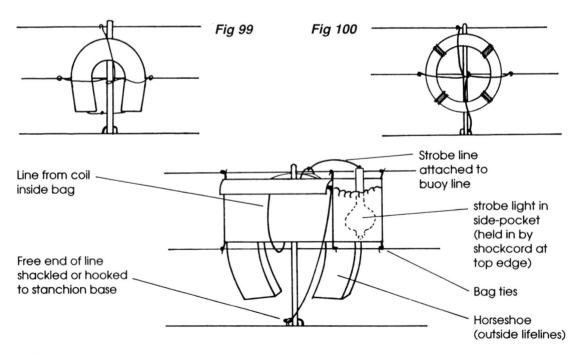

**Fig 99**

**Fig 100**

Line from coil inside bag

Strobe line attached to buoy line

strobe light in side-pocket (held in by shockcord at top edge)

Free end of line shackled or hooked to stanchion base

Bag ties

Horseshoe (outside lifelines)

**Fig 101**

# Mast Boot

*What you will need*

Clear plastic sheet (for the pattern)
Masking tape
Neoprene, PVC or car-tyre inner tube
Insulating tape
Marking pen
Contact glue
UV-resistant acrylic cloth
Thin foam (1cm thickness or less)
Velcro or open-ended zipper
Polyester webbing (1.5cm and 2.5cm width)
3mm cord
Tailor's chalk, pins, tacking thread and double-sided tape.

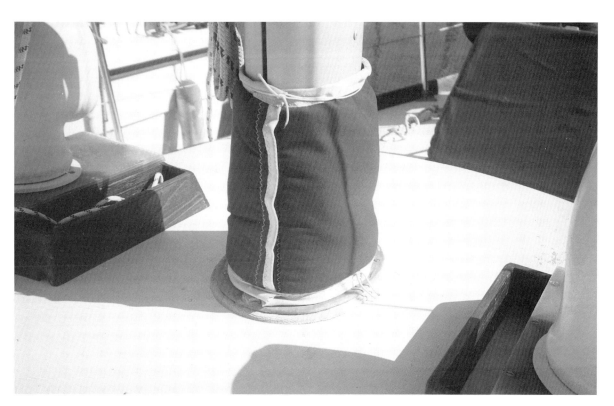

*A mast boot cover is pleasing to the eye and also a sensible protection against the elements.*

A mast boot is essential on a keel-stepped mast to prevent water running down into the interior of the boat. It should be made in two separate pieces; the inner one from waterproof material such as neoprene, PVC or rubber and the outer from UV-resistant Acrylic. To obtain a smooth, close fit, make a pattern first from clear plastic sheeting.

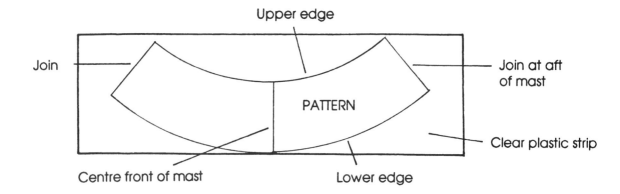

**Fig 102**

Draw a line around the mast at the upper point of the boot with a marker pen or use a strip of masking tape. Cut a piece of clear plastic 25% longer and wider than the measurement round the bottom and tape the centre of the lower edge to the centre of the front of the mast. Then tape the centre of the upper edge to the mast and pull it tight. Wrap the plastic round the mast and tape the join. Because of the different circumferences at upper and lower edge, there will be extra plastic at the lower edge of the join, and at the upper edge of the centre front. Mark off round the exact lines, and trim the plastic along these lines. At the aft centre point of the mast, draw a vertical line and cut down it. The pattern should now resemble Fig 102.

Cut out the pattern and try it again. If the fit is not exact, trim off any excess or add strips where necessary.

When cutting the pattern, add 1cm onto the joining edges on each side to allow for a 2cm overlap. Lay the pattern onto the neoprene or inner cover material, cut round it (not forgetting the overlap allowances), and tape it in place round the mast. Using contact-glue, stick the edges of the join together. When this is dry, tape around the top and bottom tightly, overlapping the upper edge so that the tape is half on the material and half on the mast. For this, the best tape is good quality wide insulating or duct tape. Two or three turns wound round as tight as possible should be sufficient.

For the outer cover, use the same pattern. If you want a padded outer cover (as shown in the photograph), you will need two pieces of fabric and a strip of thin foam (1cm thickness or less).

Lay the pattern onto the foam and mark round it. Cut it out exactly to the mark without any allowance for overlap at the join. For the inside, lay the pattern onto the wrong side of the cloth and mark round it, adding 1.5cm to each overlap side and 1cm more to both overlap edges, to allow for the bulk of the foam.

Fold all three cut out pieces in half and mark the centre lines. With the outer and inner cloths laid wrong sides together and the foam between, match the centre lines and lower edges. Pin or tack the centre lines, then machine down it using the longest straight stitch possible.

Match the sides of the inner and outer cloth, and tack them together, then curl the mast boot inwards so that you can tack evenly around the upper and lower edges.

To hold the join closed, use either an open-ended zip (with a plastic puller) or a strip of 2cm wide Velcro, either of which should be stuck in position or tacked on before sewing.

Velcro is better, but if using a zip, make sure that the open end is at the upper edge and 1cm down from it (to allow for the webbing reinforcement).

Stitch the inner half first, then fold the boot round the mast to mark the position of the other half onto the outside. (Fig 103)

To reinforce each side, cut a strip of 1.5cm wide webbing and fold it in half lengthwise. Tack it in place over the cut edge and then machine it at inner and outer edges. (Fig 104)

At the upper and lower edges use 2.5cm webbing attached in the same way, trimming off the overlap ends with a hot-knife or soldering iron. (Fig 105)

At the upper and lower edges of the centre front, sew on a length of 3mm cord 2½ times the circumference

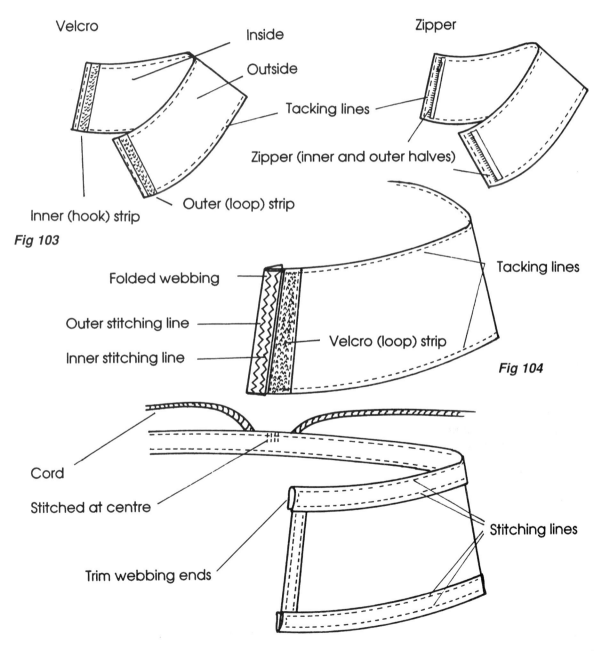

Velcro

Inside

Outside

Tacking lines

Zipper

Zipper (inner and outer halves)

Inner (hook) strip

Outer (loop) strip

**Fig 103**

Folded webbing

Outer stitching line

Inner stitching line

Velcro (loop) strip

Tacking lines

**Fig 104**

Cord

Stitched at centre

Trim webbing ends

Stitching lines

**Fig 105**

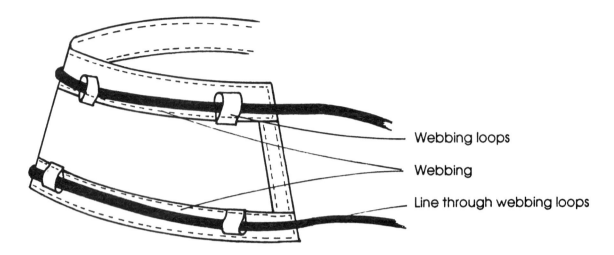

Webbing loops

Webbing

Line through webbing loops

**Fig 106**

This will allow the lines to pass twice round and leave enough to tie it securely. (If you think it necessary, when putting the webbing on top and bottom, you could slide thinner loops underneath at every quarter to run the lines through. (Fig 106)

An alternative (but not so secure) method of fastening the upper and lower edges is to glue a strip of Velcro round the mast and stitch the other corresponding half to the mast boot. But since Velcro does not stand up well to the sun, 3mm line will last longer.

# Winch Covers

*What you will need*

UV-proof material
Elastic
Drawing compasses, tape measure, double-sided tape and tailor's chalk

Winches, like any other mechanical device on a boat, need regular servicing – taking apart, checking and greasing – to ensure that they run smoothly. Protection from dust, salt and grit, when they are not in use, will cut down on maintenance and prolong their working life.

The best form of protection is a fitted cover for each winch with a hold-fast band inside to prevent them blowing off in a gale of wind. When not in use they are easily stowed inside each other in a cockpit locker.

If the upper winch drum is almost the same size as the winch base, follow this procedure.

For the top, cut a circle of cloth the same size as the diameter of the base plus 2cm.(This allows for 1cm seam allowance all round.) Use a pair of drawing compasses to obtain a perfect circle for the cutting line, then close them up 1cm to draw the stitching line. If possible, cut round the outer line with a hot-knife or flat bladed soldering iron to seal the edge.

For the body of the cover, measure round the base (plus 2cm) and from the lower edge of the base to the top of the drum, adding 2cm to the lower edge for a hem and 1cm to the upper edge of the seam. (Fig 107)

The winch cover in position.

The elastic 'hold-fast'

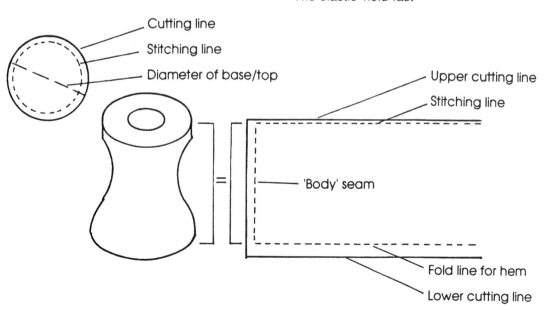

**Fig 107**

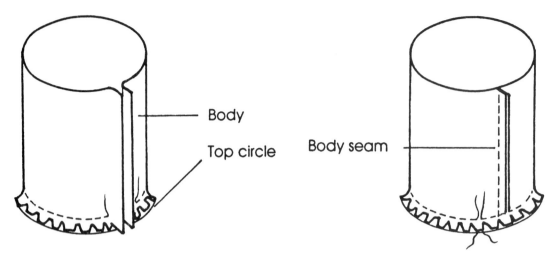

**Figs 108 and 109**

With a hot-knife or sharp scissors, make small cuts along the top edge, about 1cm apart and 5.5mm deep. Be careful not to cut beyond the stitching line.

To fasten the body to the top, either stick a strip of double-sided tape round the outer edge of the circle (on the right side) and, starting just inside the seam line, match the body edge to the top circle by stretching the cuts open – or pin the edges together and tack round the stitching line. Using a zig-zag stitch, sew round the edges, then turn the machine to straight-stitch and sew round the inner (stitching) line stopping just short of the seam line. (Fig 108)

Match the body seam edges to fit the top, pin them together and stitch the body together.

Press the seam allowance to one side and finish off the upper seaming. (Fig 109)

Press the seam allowance between the top and body into the top, fold the cover over to allow you to stitch on the right side, and zig-zag round the top close to the seam; this will hold the seam allowance in place and make for a neat finish. (Fig 110)

Try the cover to check the lower edge, then turn the hem under, crease it along the fold, and stitch down the inner and outer edges. (Fig 111)

One third of the way down the body seam, stitch a loop of elastic onto the seam allowance. This loop, when stretched, should be just long enough to pass over the upper winch drum and fit snugly round the waist of the winch.

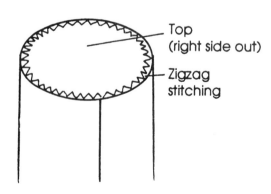

**Fig 110**

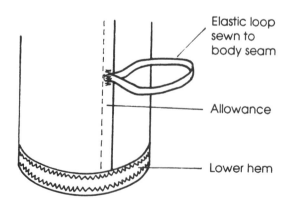

**Fig 111**

*The cover inside-out as at Fig111.*

To put the cover on, first slip the elastic over, then slide the cover 'body' over the upper drum and down until it fits snugly over the base.

If the top of the winch is considerably smaller than the base, and you want the cover to fit neatly, the body will have to be cut on a curve, with the upper edge the same circumference measurement as the upper drum (plus the seam allowances).

The simplest way to obtain the exact shape for the body is to make a pattern out of clear plastic. Wrap a strip of this round the winch and hold it with masking tape. With a marker pen, draw round the upper and lower edges and cut the vertical seam lines where they meet. Having made the pattern, add 1cm to the upper edge, 2cm to the lower edge for the hem, and 1.5cm to each side of the vertical seam. The height of the base will determine the shape of the body. (Fig 112)

Attach the body to the top and finish as before.

Winch covers when not in use, can be stowed one inside another, preferably with your sail covers to remind you to put them on!

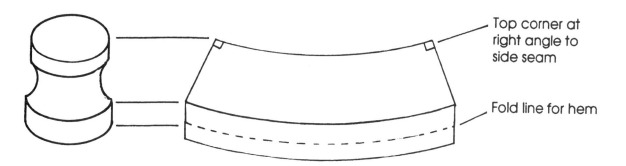

Top corner at right angle to side seam

Fold line for hem

**Fig 112**

# Hatch Covers

*What you will need*

UV-proof material
2mm leech-line or thin cord
2 No1 grommets or 4 snap studs
Tape measure, tailor's chalk, double-sided adhesive tape.

*Hatch covers keep the sun from the interior but allow the hatch to be opened to let fresh air below.*

Perspex or plexi-glass hatch tops will, as does much else on a boat, be subjected to damage by exposure to the sun, weather and general wear. So, to protect them and prolong their useful life, it is worthwhile making fitted covers for each one from UV-resistant material. If you can match the material to that which has already been used for sail covers and dodgers, they will add to the look of a 'well cared for yacht'.

On most modern boats, the hatches are almost flush with the deck, hinged on the forward side with closing handles aft and angled slightly outwards at the base of each corner. (Fig 113)

To calculate the fabric, measure from the deck over the hatch, fore and aft. (Include any hinges and handles that protrude from the main profile.) Then measure the athwartship dimensions. Add 2cm each side of the hem and this will give the total cloth measurements. Chalk this on the wrong side of the material and then measure the hatch top. Mark this by centring it with a line drawn from corner to corner. (Fig 114)

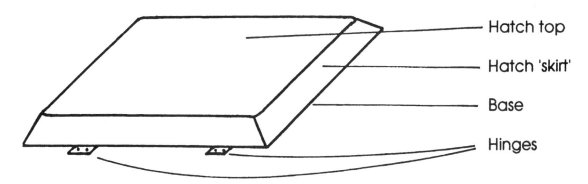

**Fig 113**

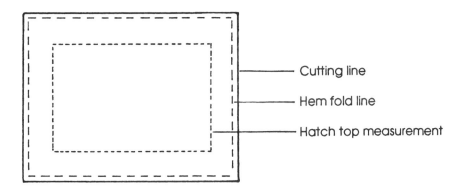

Cutting line

Hem fold line

Hatch top measurement

**Fig 114**

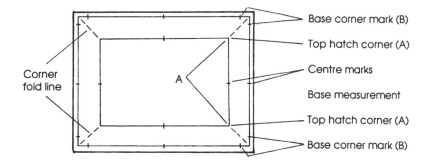

Base corner mark (B)

Top hatch corner (A)

Centre marks

Base measurement

Top hatch corner (A)

Base corner mark (B)

Corner fold line

A

**Fig 115**

Measure the base sides, and by halving them mark the base corners on the fold lines. (Fig 115)

Taking one corner at a time, crease the corner fold mark, matching the cut edges. Draw a line from A (corner of hatch top) to B (base corner mark) and straight-stitch down it to the fold line, then in the same angle, reinforcing (by reverse stitching) each end. Cut off the excess material 1cm outside the stitching line. (Fig 116)

Clip the seam allowance open at B, and press the seam open. Turn the hem up along the fold line and crease it in place (but don't stitch it yet).

Lay the cover over the hatch and mark the position of the hinges and handles. These will need to be cut out and reinforced before sewing down the hem. The strongest method is to use doubled over webbing or wide bias-tape. (Fig 117)

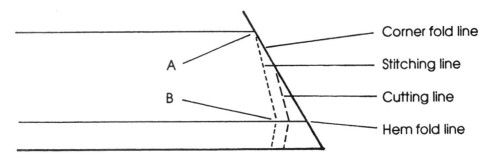

**Fig 116**

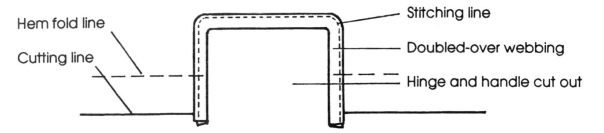

**Fig 117**

Trim off the reinforcing at the cutting line, turn over the material at the fold line and zig-zag stitch along the cut edge (inner) to form a hem.

Run a length of cord from the outer hinge turn-over through the hem, through the handle cut outs, to emerge at the other hinge cut out. Stitch the cord in place either side of the handle cut out and leave 10cm of cord free at each end.

Through the hem between the hinges thread a short length of cord (with a protruding loop at each end) and stitch it in place at the centre. (Fig 118)

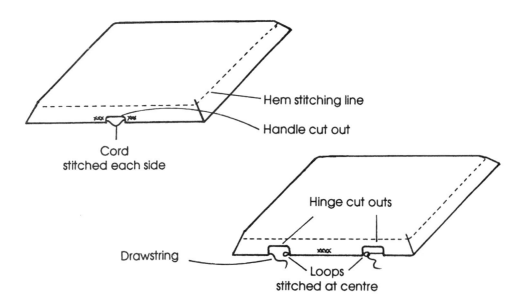

**Fig 118**

*The closed hatch with the cover secured so that it will not be blown away if the wind pipes up.*

This method ensures that with the front cord tucked under the hinges (fastened through the loops) and the aft cords under the handle, the cover cannot blow off and yet the main drawstring can be pulled tight for a close fit.

The cover can, if wanted, be left in place permanently, although care must be taken (when closing the hatch) that it is not trapped between hatch and deck.

## Older Hatches

On hatches of an older type, with a raised wooden edge set on a varnished coaming, it may be easier (and less wasteful on material) to cut the top piece separate from the skirt.

If the top overlaps the coaming, lay the material over it and mark round from underneath. Add 1cm on each side for the seam allowance. For the skirt, measure round the hatch base and add 5cm (1cm each end for the join, with 3cm extra error margin), then the required depth, allowing 1cm at the upper edge (seam allowance) and 2cm at the lower edge for the hem. To stitch top to skirt, put the right sides together and starting at the centre of one top side (2cm in from the skirt join), straight-stitch along to the first corner. Snip the skirt seam allowance here to avoid it puckering around the corner. (Fig 119)

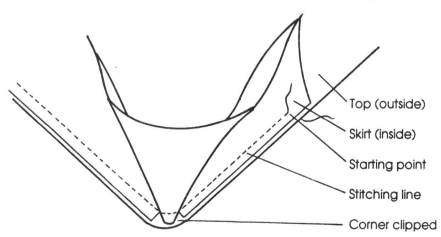

Top (outside)

Skirt (inside)

Starting point

Stitching line

Corner clipped

**Fig 119**

Continue stitching along each side, clipping the corners as you come to them. When you have almost reached the starting point, cut the thread and match the two skirt edges so that when joined, trimmed off and pressed open, they will lie flat to the top. Now finish the top/skirt seam join. (Fig 120)

Press the top/skirt seam allowance to the inside (towards the top) and, from the outside, zig-zag stitch round the top close to the seam for a neater and stronger finish. (Fig 121)

Turn the hem under and stitch it down at the inner (cut) edge only if you want to run a drawstring through. If so, before you stitch, insert two grommets just above the fold line on the outside

at the centre of one side, to allow the drawstring to be pulled from outside. (Fig 122)

If you prefer to fasten the cover in place with snap-studs, sew both inner and outer edges of the hem. Put the cover in place and tack it on with a spike at each corner. (This will give you the position for the studs on the wood and cover.) Screw the male studs to the wood first, then put one female to the cover, to check the position of the others before inserting them. It may also be advisable to mark the skirt on the aft edge, in case it is not reversible.

There are many different types of hatch, but these ideas can easily be adapted to fit most designs.

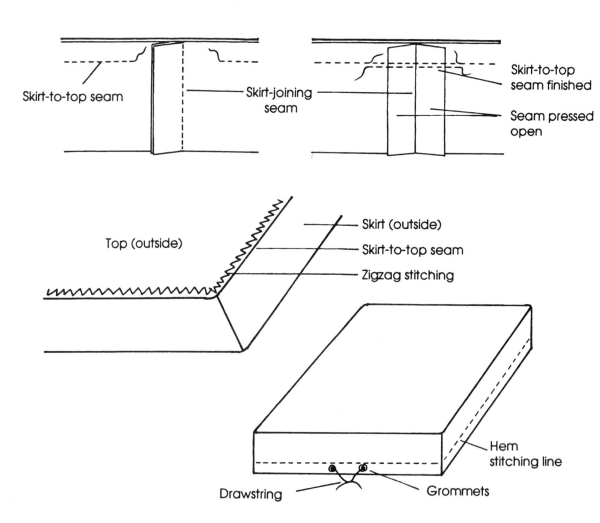

**Figs 120, 121 and 122**

# The Windjammer

A simple and effective way to tame and stow your spinnaker or cruising chute.

*What you will need*

Lightweight nylon fabric
A piece of PVC
4mm braidline (for the uphaul/downhaul and cross-line at the top)
Shock-cord
Bronze brazing rod, joining sleeve and reinforced hose or heavy duty, non-flexible cable.
2.5cm and 12mm wide webbing
4 No 1 brass or stainless grommets
1 small nylon/plastic thimble
8mm braidline
2 larger thimbles
A small block
A long narrow shackle
Tailor's chalk, pins, thread, straight-edge, double-sided tape,
needle and waxed thread, an iron and scissors.

*The Windjammer in the process of smothering a spinnaker prior to dropping it completely.*

There are many different versions of spinnaker socks and snuffers. Almost every well-known sailmaker has designed and named his own variation. The basic concept on almost every design is, however, the same. A tube of cloth is pulled down over the sail to collapse it very quickly, thus taking the panic out of the drop when, inevitably, the wind has piped up. On the hoist, the sail can be raised in the form of a tame sausage and fine adjustments made at leisure before the sail is broken open. The sock remains above the head of the sail, concertina-like out of harm's way and ready for instant use. Some designs are more complicated than others, but here is a suggestion, simple enough to be made by any average sailor.

The first consideration is the choice of fabric. Lightweight nylon provides a good solution, not necessarily the rip-stop used for the sail itself, but any colourfast material that will compress well when the Windjammer has been hoisted above the setting sail. The fabric does not have to be UV-proofed since it is unlikely that you will be sailing with a spinnaker for days on end.

The first step is to measure the forestay and then deduct 75cm. Then measure the circumference of the bunched sail between the clews. If the latter measurement is less than half the width of the material it is worth cutting the cloth in half lengthwise and then joining the two strips to give the required length.

If there are to be one or more joins in the cloth, it is important to make sure that they lie flat, with no fraying edges to snag the sail. The simplest method is to lay the cloth, right sides together, with a 1cm gap between the edges to be joined and straight-stitch 1cm inside the lower edge (Fig 123)

Turn the upper edge over to the seam line and press it down. Open out the body of the cloth and iron the seam allowance so that the turnover is hiding the raw edge. Run a line of zig-zag stitching along the turnover and through the outer cloth to hold the seam in place and flat. (Fig 124)

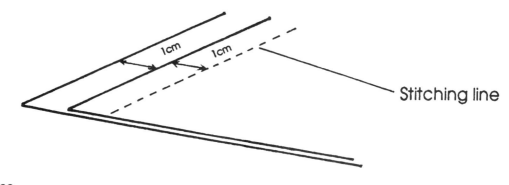

**Fig 123**

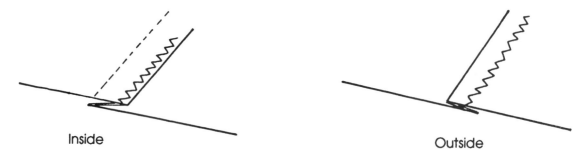

Inside                    Outside

**Fig 124**

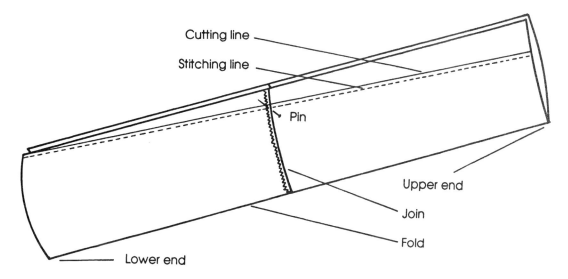

**Fig 125**

This will create a reinforced, smooth inner join which will barely show on the outside if you have been able to match the thread colour to the cloth. Now fold the cloth in half along the length. If you have used contrasting panels, pin each join so that the seams meet exactly. (If you have used the same colour material throughout, and the thread matches, this is not so important, but matching the joins will make for a more professional looking job.)

To mark the lengthwise stitching line, remember that the top circumference does not have to be as large as the lower stiffened circle. On almost any spinnaker, the reinforced head-patch will be less in circumference than the bunched sail at the lower end, but since the purpose of the Windjammer is to compress the sail, the lower circle must be large enough to clear the head without catching.

Therefore, with the cloth folded in half, the stitching line will not be quite parallel to the fold. The top measurement can be 30% less than the lower end. (Fig 125)

Cut the material 2cm outside the stitching line. Chalk in a mark 1cm up from the lower edge on the stitching line and 26cm up on the fold line, and draw a smooth curve between the marks. (The raised front will enable the windjammer when lowered, to slide easily down the bunt of the sail.) (Fig 126)

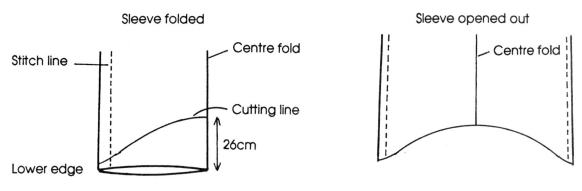

**Fig 126**

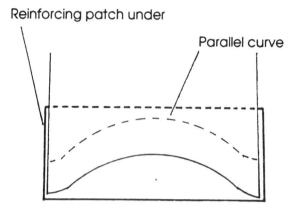

Reinforcing patch under

Parallel curve

**Fig 127**

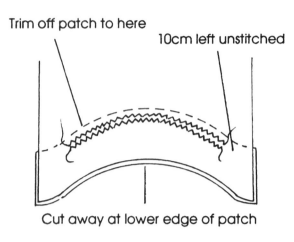

Trim off patch to here

10cm left unstitched

Cut away at lower edge of patch

**Fig 128**

Cut along the curved line, open the cloth out flat and draw a parallel curve 7cm up on the outside. Lay a flat piece of strong material, such as PVC (the width of the sleeve and 35cm high) onto the underside of the opened-out sleeve as a reinforced facing piece for the stiffening ring. (Fig 127)

Run two lines of zig-zag stitching close together just inside the upper line, leaving 10cm open at each end. Trim off the excess heavy material from the inside, close to the upper row of stitching, and cut away to match up with the lower edge of the cloth. (Fig 128)

Fold the cloth, right sides together, along the centre line matching the long edges and all the cross-seams. Sew along the stitching line with a fairly long straight-stitch, being careful not to catch the edges of the lower reinforcing panel.

Draw a chalk line across the stitching line 8cm up from the lower edge, at then at every 35cm up to the top with the final mark being 15cm from the top edge (to allow for the hem). These marks are for the placing of the webbing loops through which the inner(uphaul) line will run. Don't worry if it does not come out exactly. An extra loop at the upper end is a help. Count the marks and cut the equivalent number of webbing strips; 12mm wide webbing, 6cm long.

Fold each strip in half and pin it to the mark, 1cm over the line of stitching with the loop towards the fold. (Fig 129)

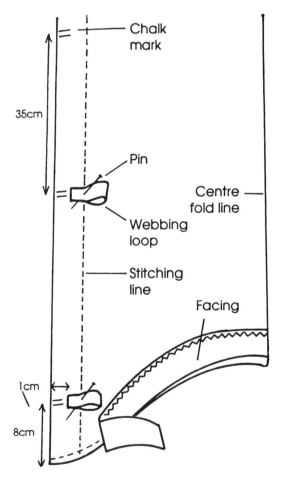

Chalk mark

35cm

Pin

Centre fold line

Webbing loop

Stitching line

Facing

1cm

8cm

**Fig 129**

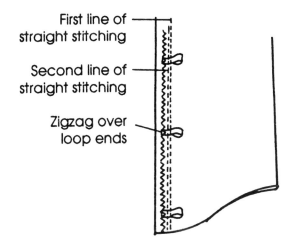

First line of straight stitching

Second line of straight stitching

Zigzag over loop ends

**Fig 130**

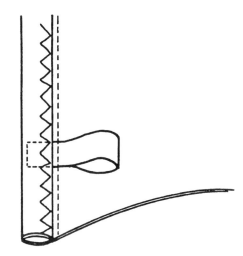

**Fig 131**

Run another line of straight-stitching down the length of the cloth, just inside the previous one to hold the loops in place, and another row of zig-zag stitching just outside to anchor the ends of the loops. (Fig 130)

Turn the edges of the material towards the seam over the webbing ends and zig-zag down to hold it in place. (Fig 131)

Spreading out the lower edge, line up the seam stitching line with the centre-fold line. Press the turned-over seam to the right to lie over the first webbing loop. From just above this point, zig-zag down the seam to the bottom edge.

To finish the upper edge of the facing, lay it flat over the seam with the ends overlapping and sew down each short edge. Then finish off the two lines of zig-zag around the upper edge. (Fig 132)

To finish off the upper end, mark a line around and 5cm down (this is the first fold) and another line 5cm below the first for the second fold. Crease or iron the first fold to the inside, then turn the second fold over, and pin or tack it along the lower edge. Machine (zig-zag) along the lower edge, leaving a gap of 5cm at the centre fold line. Run another row of zig-zag all around the upper edge. Half-way between the two lines, put another row of zig-zag with a break at the same point as in the lower line.

At the half-way mark between the seam and the centre fold on each side, knock in a grommet between the lower and middle lines of stitching. (Fig 133)

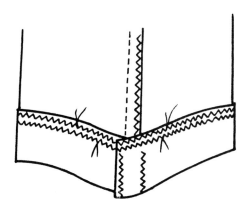

**Fig 132**

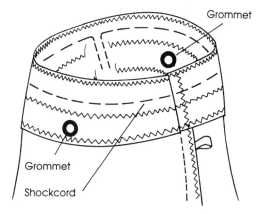

Grommet

Grommet

Shockcord

**Fig 133**

Using a large safety-pin, run a length of 3mm shock-cord through the gaps in the lower two lines of stitching and around the top, below the uppermost line. Pull it tight enough to gather the top and stitch the ends together. Zig-zag over the breaks in the lower two lines of stitching.

There are several ways to make the stiffener at the lower edge. It must be strong enough to keep a circular shape, but not too heavy or awkward to handle and stow. After experimenting (with plastic conduit tube, heavy rigging wire, the rim of a plastic bucket etc.) I found that a 5mm bronze brazing rod (run through a length of tight-fitting reinforcing hose) would bend to the perfect circle, with ends joined through a copper sleeve and soldered together.

To find the length, take the measurement from the seam around the lower edge and back to the seam. Cut the rod to this length, slide the hose (with a 10cm slit along the length at one end to allow for the join in the rod) over it, and bend it into a circle. Slip the sleeve onto one end, push the other end in and solder both ends of the sleeve to the rod. If the inside diameter of the hose allows, slide it over the join in the rod and tape the split ends together at the opposite side. Try the final fit before you solder to ensure that the whole issue will fit inside the hem. Too tight a fit is not desired since you still must reinforce the bottom edge.

Once you have the circle fitted, push it between the two layers of cloth and tack it up close to the upper row of stitching as possible. Then pin or tack the two lower edges of cloth together. If your machine can handle it, run a line of zig-zag around the lower edge and a line of straight stitching just above. If not, sew the edges together by hand; a blanket-stitch with a back stitch above will hold.

For the necessary reinforcement and for a neat and practical finish, take a length of 2.5cm webbing folded in half along the length, and sew it over the raw edge, with the join overlapping at the seam. This will offer extra strength to the up/downhaul line.

When the stiffener is fixed in place, put a grommet just above and just below it on the seam. (These are the fixing points for the continuous uphaul/downhaul line.) (See photo)

*The position of the two grommets for the uphaul/downhaul in the bottom neck of the windjammer.*

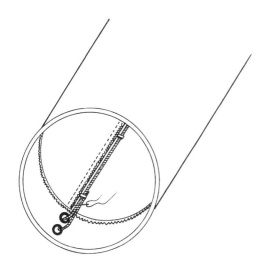

**Fig 134**

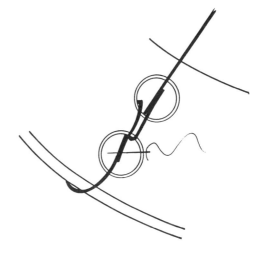

**Fig 135**

For the up/downhaul line you will need 4–5mm braidline twice the length of the sleeve plus 5 metres and also a small block. Take one end of the line over the block and down the inside of the sleeve through the webbing loops. At the bottom, pass it through the upper grommet, around the stiffener and back through the lower grommet. Lay the end alongside the line and stitch them together (Fig 134)

Run the other end of the line down the outside, through the bottom grommet from the inside, round the stiffener and back to the inside through the upper grommet. Stitch the end to the line as

before. (Fig 135)

At the upper end of the sleeve, take a short length of the same sized line and seize a thimble into it at the centre. Run the ends through the grommets each side (from the outside) and stitch them to the line. (Fig 136)

To fasten the block to the top (cross-line) thimble, use a long narrow shackle (or a stain-less-steel link shackle). (Fig 137)

Either of these will pass through the becket of the block and through the thimble with enough clearance for the up/downhaul to run freely. (Fig 138)

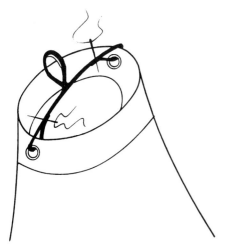

**Fig 136**

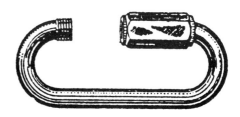

**Fig 137**

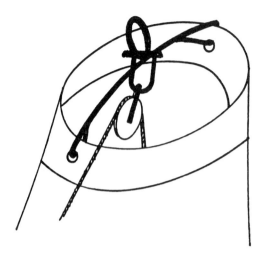

**Fig 138**

To attach the spinnaker at the head, a rope strop is required of about 50cm to 1 metre long (depending on the length of the forestay ) with a thimble seized in at both ends. (The strop should be just long enough for the sleeve to concertina

above the head of the sail. Shackle the lower end of the strop to the swivel at the head of the sail. If the sail does not have a swivel, either attach one – with four turns of 2.5cm webbing – or use a swivel-eye boat snap, fastened to the sail, that can hook onto the head-eye. It is important to have a swivel at the head to stop the sail twisting.

The top end of the strop should pass through the sleeve on the opposite side of the cross-line to the seam. Lie the strop eye to the cross line thimble and join them with a shackle large enough to accommodate the snap-shackle on the halyard.

To set the Windjammer, hoist the sail on a quiet windless day, with the sleeve pulled up (and the sheets attached – just in case!) Shake out the folds in the foot and pull on the downhaul. Lower the sleeve over the sail, drop the halyard and fold the Windjammer with the sail inside. Tie a line around and stow it ready for instant use.

With the sail hoisted, the Windjammer nestles above the head near the top of the forestay.

*The Windjammer pulled down over a cruising chute.*

# Seachute – A Simplified Sea Anchor

*What you will need*

8–10oz sailcloth
2.5cm webbing
5cm webbing
No 1 grommets
6mm braidline
Open-end stainless-steel thimble
Swivel-eye boat snap
Hot-knife or soldering iron
Tailor's chalk
Pushpins, compasses and pins

A sea anchor or drogue, is one of the emergency items that you hope never to use. Like the storm jib and trysail, it will probably be stowed in the most inaccessible locker to allow space for more frequently used gear. But when you need it you will want to lay your hands on it fast and know that it is ready for instant use.

The older designs, with a wire or metal ring around the mouth of the drogue, take up more space and are generally harder to handle than the later 'parachute' models which are equally effective.

These 'parachute' types can be as simple or as complicated as you choose to make them. Here is a design for a model that is quick and easy to make , stows in its own bag in less space than a large bath towel and can be attached to a warp and streamed in seconds.

The best material to use is heavy sailcloth (8–10oz) rather than canvas. Sailcloth will saturate almost as fast (to allow it to sink), dry more quickly, last longer and stow in a smaller space. The size of the 'Seachute' will depend on the length of the boat. Since you start by cutting a circle, a rough guide to measuring the diameter is 10cm diameter per metre of hull length. When finished, this will be approximately the suggested Admiralty formula. For multihulls, double the diameter.

The simplest way to mark the circle onto the cloth is to use a piece of string, a pencil and a pushpin. Tie the string loosely at the lower end of the pencil and knot the string at the measurement of the radius (half the diameter).

Lay the cloth out flat on a wooden surface; with the pin at the centre and the string fully extended, draw your circle. Cut round this line, if possible with a hot-knife to seal the edge.

Fold the circle in half, then in quarters and crease the fold lines lightly with the blunt edge of your cutting shears so that the centre point and quarter lines show clearly.

Cut a small circle (approx 20cm diameter) of the same or stronger weight, but colour contrasting cloth, as a reinforcing patch. Match the centres and quarter lines and stitch it to the larger circle on the outer side.

Cut one quarter out from the complete circle, just inside the crease lines to leave 1cm on each side as a turn-over. (Fig 139)

Using a compass, mark a circle around the centre 10cm in diameter and another 1cm outside this. The first is the cutting line and the second is the sewing line for the webbing reinforcement.

This will form the 'spill-hole' at the narrow end, which is necessary to prevent the chute from oscillating when streamed.

Stitch round just inside the sewing line to hold the edges together and cut out the centre along the cutting line. (Fig 140)

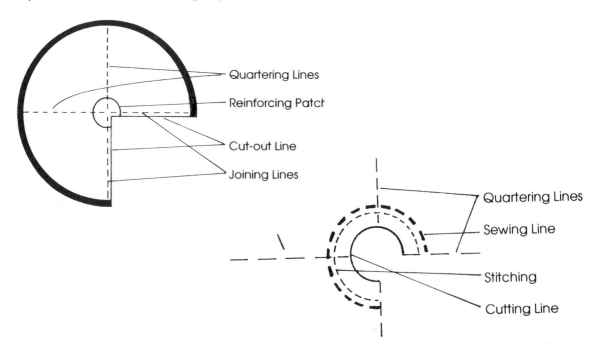

Quartering Lines

Reinforcing Patch

Cut-out Line

Joining Lines

Quartering Lines

Sewing Line

Stitching

Cutting Line

**Figs 139**                                    **Fig 140**

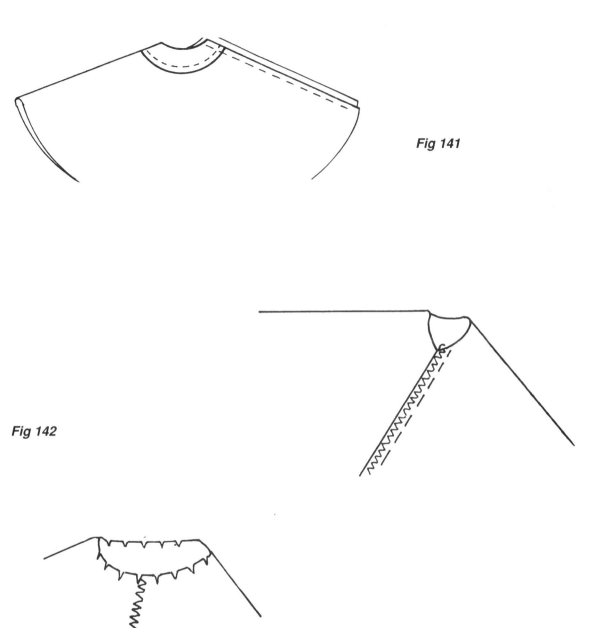

**Fig 141**

**Fig 142**

**Fig 143**

Fold the 'Seachute' in half, with the right sides together, matching the cutting lines at the centre and outer edges. (Fig 141)

Straight-stitch along the sewing line and press the seams to one side. From the outside, zig-zag stitch over the seam allowance to reinforce the seam and hold it in place. (Fig 142)

You will now need a short length of 2.5cm wide webbing, heat-sealed at both ends, to reinforce the narrow (aft) end. This will be easier to stitch on if the cloth is 'nicked' at 1cm intervals around the edge. (Fig 143)

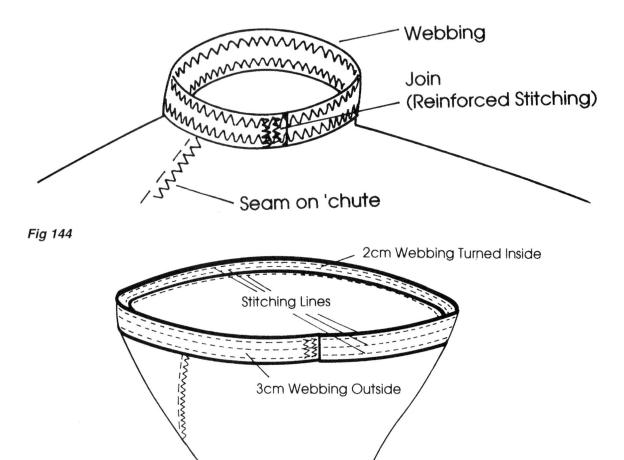

**Fig 144**

**Fig 145**

The webbing should be folded in half and stuck or tacked in place before stitching, with the ends overlapping by at least 1cm. Stitch it round with two rows of zig-zag stitching, reinforcing the overlap. (Fig 144)

At the other end of the chute, mark a line 3cm in, all round. Take a length of 5cm wide webbing to match plus enough to allow for a 2cm overlap join at the ends. Stitch one side of the webbing to the line, reinforcing the overlap, then turn the other side over the chute edge and machine round it. (For accuracy and even stitching, tack it in place first.) Now sew round the outer edge. From the outside, you should have three rows of zig-zag stitching showing on the webbing and two on the inside. (Fig 145)

Fold the chute in half at the join. Mark the

webbing at the opposite point and at one third intervals between these marks, giving six attachment points around the edge. At each mark insert a No 1 grommet between the outer and central stitching lines.

Measure the length of the seam on the chute, double it and add 20cm. Cut three lengths of 6mm braidline to this length and stitch them together at the centre.

Push the thimble over the swivel eye of a boat-snap, so that the wider upper end lies on the swivel eye. (Fig 146)

Pass the three ends of the braidline through the swivel over the thimble, and matching the centre of the lines to the top of the thimble, stitch them together firmly in place at the lower end. (Fig 147)

**Fig 146**

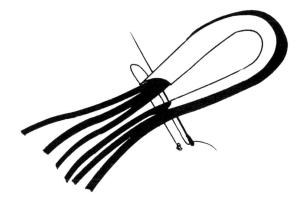

**Fig 147**

Fasten the snap-hook to a point high enough to allow the lines to dangle freely and making sure that they are all equal in length and not twisted at the top, tie each one to its appropriate grommet with a round turn and two half hitches, seizing the free end to the line above the knot. (Fig 148)

The 'Seachute' has been extensively tested at sea. The one in the photograph was thrown over the stern of a Carter 33 which was sailing at six knots. Within seconds the boat speed reduced to less than half a knot.

For recovery purposes, a trip line is not recommended as it could tangle around the drogue warp, fouling both warp and trip line. It is better to tie a small fender (coloured red) or an orange fishing float buoy, with 5m of 3mm line, to a grommet through the reinforcing patch at the narrow end of the chute and just inside the webbing. In this way, when the emergency is over and if you cannot pull in the chute, the warp can be released from the boat and picked up later with a boat hook. There is little chance of a float streamed like this tangling with the warp as it will stream aft of the chute and be pulled under by the load but surface when set free.

If you use a very heavy warp it may be sensible to add another fender at the boat end of the warp before cutting free.

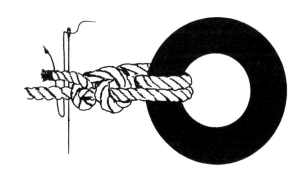

**Fig 148**

*In tests this 'Seachute' slowed a 33 foot boat from six knots to half a knot within seconds.*

## 'Seachute' Stow Bag

*What you will need*

Nylon Cloth
2mm cord

For the size, crease the chute lengthwise between the grommets and roll the excess cloth around it and over the lines. Measure the length and circumference. Cut a rectangle of cloth 5cm larger on two sides, fold it in half and machine along the length and lower edge. Turn the upper edge over 3cm and stitch the inner hem, leaving a 1cm gap either side of the seam to run a draw-string through. (Fig 149)

Turn the bag right side out, knot the ends of the cord together and mark 'Seachute' on the outside.

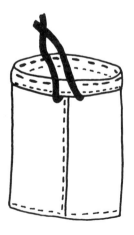

**Fig 149**

# A Summer Awning or a Winter Tent

*What you will need*

UV-resistant material
6mm braided rope
2 poles
No 1 grommets
3mm cord for tie-downs

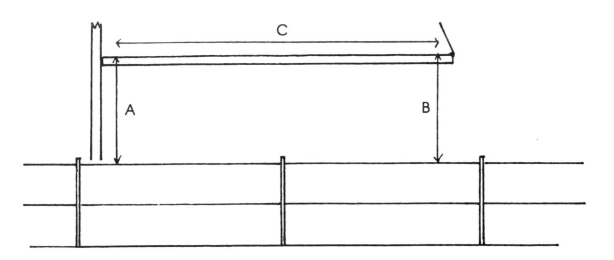

**Fig 150**

If you are to spend a lot of time in a sunny climate, some form of protection is a must. Here is an idea for a sun-awning that can also double as a winter tent.

With the boom at its normal level when not under sail (provided there is adequate space below it) and on the centreline of the boat running fore and aft, measure the distance between it and the top lifeline at a point 10cm back from the mast (A). Take the same distance 10cm forward of the topping-lift (B) and the measurement between these two points on the boom (C). (Fig 150)

The most suitable material for the job is water and UV-resistant acrylic. Unless you are lucky enough to find some twice the width of measurement A, you must use two lengths joined at the centre (C).

Add 10cm to each end of the rectangle, 1cm to the length one side and 4cm to the length at the other. (Fig 151) The top corners AC and BC should be square and if possible the line at D should be placed on the selvedge of the fabric.

Fold a piece of material a little longer than the total length (including the hems at each end) in half, pinning or stapling the long edge at the top together, and cut it out. (Fig 152)

**Fig 151**

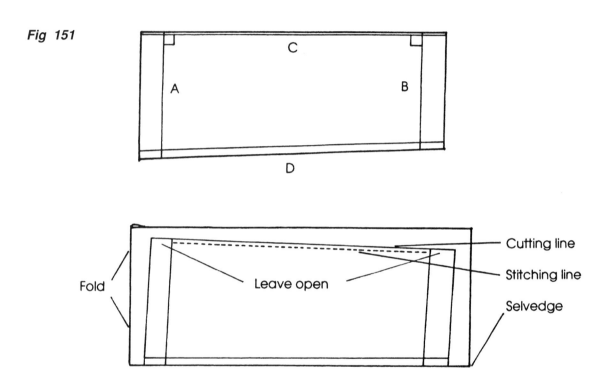

**Fig 152**

From 10cm in at each end, stitch the top edges together, reinforcing the sewing at each end by going back over the stitching two or three times. Press the seam allowance to one side and stitch along it as far as the openings at each end.

Fold the cover in half along the seam, with the wrong sides together and lay a length of 6mm braided rope into the fold, with enough emerging at the front to tie round the mast and a shorter length at the back to fasten to the topping-lift. Using a close-sewing foot on the machine, sew the rope into the fold, hand stitching through it and the cloth at each end. (Fig 153)

Fold the hems at both lower edges to the underside along the line 4cm in from the edge and stitch them in place. Turn under 1cm along the front and back edges and run a line of stitching to hold them in place.

Lay the cover flat with the wrong side uppermost, and turn the front and back edges over again to give a 9cm sleeve. Crease the fold and at the centre turn in the extra material. Sew the sleeve down twice at the inner edge. (Fig 154)

Put in a grommet at each outer corner on the fold, and three or four grommets evenly spaced along each long side.

To use your cover as a sun awning, you will need two poles 10cm. longer than the sleeves, with a hold drilled through at each end. Tie a cord to each corner grommet on the cover, insert a pole into each sleeve, and thread the corner lines through the holes at the end of each pole. (These lines will keep the awning stretched out flat and prevent the poles from working their way out.)

Lay the poles across the boom and fasten the centre back rope to the topping lift just above the sail. Take the forward rope round the mast above the top of the sailcover (to avoid chafe) and take the tension up on it until the centre seam is stretched tight. Using the lines at each corner, tie the pole ends down to the lifelines at each side (the tie-lines should be angled to fore and aft to keep the sides of the awning stretched.) For added strength use tie-lines from the grommets on the sides to attach to the lifelines.

To use the cover as a winter tent, remove the poles at each end and tie the lines at the corners and sides to the tip or bottom lifelines. If you take off the mainsail the front of the cover can be lowered, but avoid the cover touching the boom, as this will decrease the water-resistant quality and cause chafe. (Fig 155)

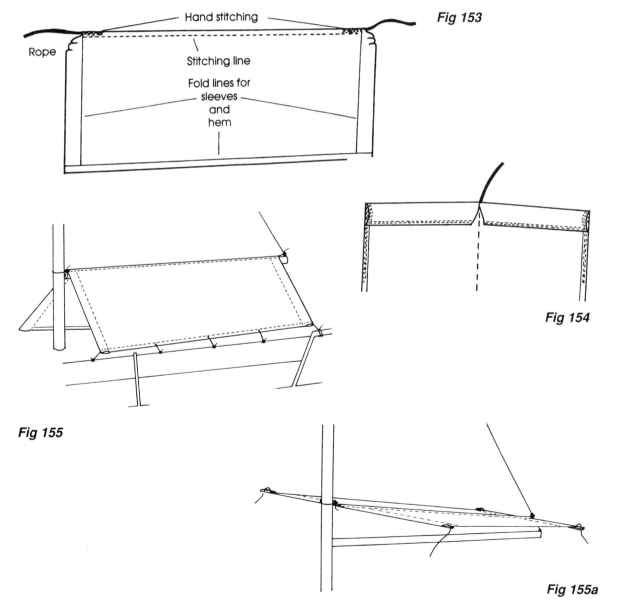

Hand stitching — *Fig 153*

Rope

Stitching line

Fold lines for
sleeves
and
hem

*Fig 154*

*Fig 155*

*Fig 155a*

# Keep Cool
# – A Multidirectional Wind-scoop

*What you will need*

Lightweight nylon fabric
2 × 1m bronze brazing rod (or thin dowel)
Tape or rubber tubing to protect the ends
12mm webbing or 3mm leechline
Snap studs or saddle-eyes and No 1 grommets
Tailor's chalk, pins, straight-edge, tape
measure, double-sided tape, an iron, scissors,
thread etc

During hot weather, life below decks can get
pretty uncomfortable without good ventilation.
One obvious answer is a wind-scoop on the
forward hatch to funnel air into the boat.
However, if the boat is moored in a marina, the
regular scoop shape wind-catcher will present a
problem, as it must be adjusted for every change
in the wind's direction.

Here is an idea for a wind-scoop that will catch
the wind from any direction and does not need
adjustment once in position.

The best and cheapest material to use is a
medium-weight nylon fabric, similar to sailbag
cloth. This is light enough to fill in a slight breeze
and soft enough not to rustle like sailcloth or rip-
stop spinnaker cloth.

The maximum effective height is approximately 1.25m, as anything taller will swing about
in the breeze and become ineffective. For the
panel size (if the hatch is square) measure from
one corner to the centre of the opposite side, and
double this measurement, adding 6cm (for a 3cm
hem on each side).

If the hatch is rectangular, measure from the
corners of one long side to the centre of the
opposite long side. (Fig 156)

You will need two pieces of material the
lengths of the corner-centre-corner (plus extra for
the hems) and the required height, to which you
must add 5cm at the top and bottom for turnovers. On both pieces, mark the fold lines all
round with chalk and turn the raw edges in to
these lines. (This is the first fold.) Press down

*Here the breeze is coming from astern.*

and turn over again at the inner (second) fold
line. This will give you a finished hem of 1,5cm
on the vertical edges and 2.5cm on the horizon-
tals. Stitch round each panel on the inner and
outer edges of the hems (Fig 157)

Fold each panel in half, matching the vertical
sides and press a crease down the centre.(Fig
158)

Lay both pieces flat, one on top of the other,
matching upper and lower edges and the centre
creases. Pin the centres together and straight-
stitch down the crease from the top, reinforcing
the lower end by reversing the stitching. At the

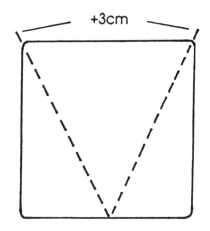

**Fig 156**

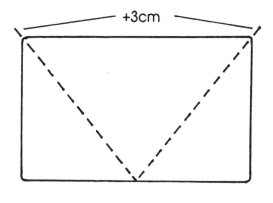

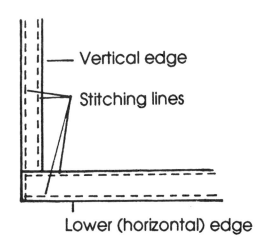

**Fig 157**

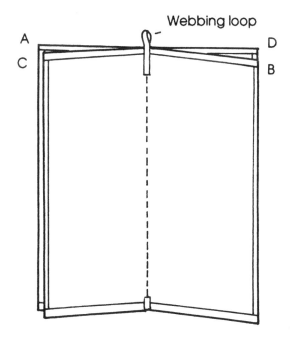

**Fig 159**

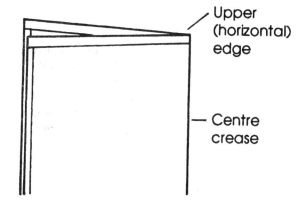

**Fig 158**

upper edge, stitch a doubled loop of 1cm wide webbing down the crease, with one end each side and the stitched ends 10cm below. (Fig 159)

Measure from one corner across the top to the opposite one; this is the finished diagonal measurement of the top of the square piece. Mark this out on the right side of the material (2nd fold line). Draw another line 3cm outside this (1st fold-line) and cut round 3cm outside this. (Fig 160)

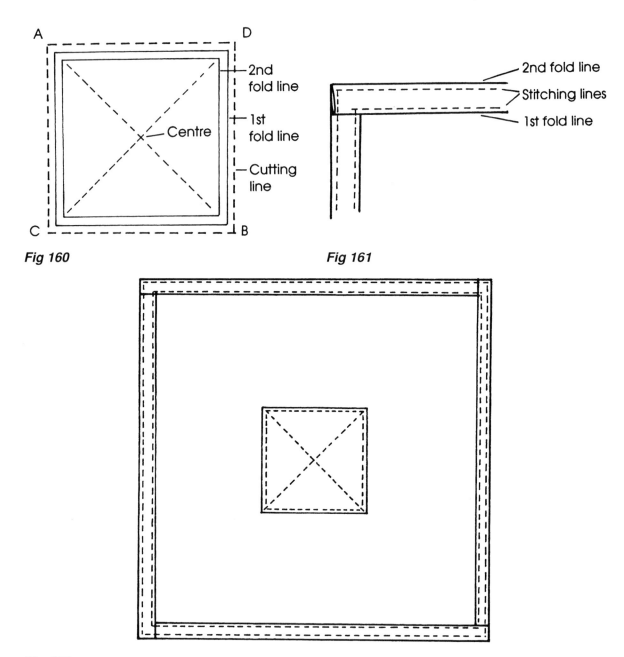

**Fig 160**

**Fig 161**

**Fig 162**

Turn under the first fold line all round and press it down. Then do the same along the second fold and sew round the inner and outer edges of the hem. (Fig 161)

Draw a line from corner to corner on the inside with chalk, to find the centre point. This will need to be strengthened by adding a patch, so cut a square piece of cloth 10cm on each side and pin, tack or stick it at the centre, matching the corners to the diagonal lines. Stitch round the edges and from corner to corner. (Fig 162)

On the outside, take a strip of 2cm wide webbing 20cm long, fold it in half and sew backwards and forwards across it 4cm down from the

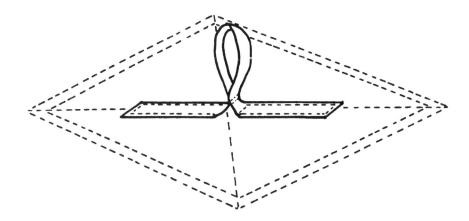

**Fig 163**

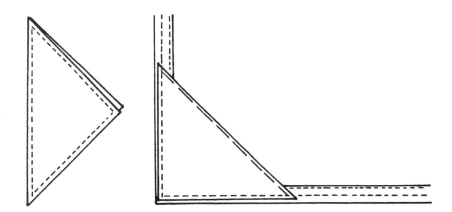

**Fig 164**

fold. Spread the ends apart and pin them along one of the diagonal stitching lines and sew them by hand or machine firmly through the patch. (Fig 163)

Turn the top over so that the underside is facing you. Cut four squares 15cm on each side and fold each diagonally. Stitch along the fold line and 5mm inside the raw edge. Turn the raw edges under, just inside the stitching line and pin each triangle to a corner of the top section on the underside. Stitch down the two short sides, leaving the fold free, to form pockets for the cross-battens. (Fig 164)

Another, possibly stronger method of making the corner pockets is to cut a strip of PVC to a width of 10cm, fold it in half along the length and lay it across the corners. Sew along the inner edge. (Fig 165)

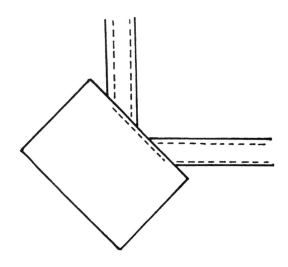

**Fig 165**

*Looking from below, this is how the top battened section should appear when complete.*

Fold the other half over, matching the edges (or if necessary overlapping them slightly to leave a bit of the corner exposed) and sew round the outer edge of the top stitching to hold the corner pockets in place. (Fig 166)

For the cross-battens, measure from corner to corner of the top – the measurements should be equal, if not, average them by adding the two lengths and dividing by two. Cut two lengths of bronze rod or dowel to this size and flatten the ends slightly, round them off and sand smooth.

With the main body of the scoop upside down and opened out so that it forms a cross, pin each corner to the top section (on the inside). Hold it up and make sure that it hangs properly, that you have pinned the outer corners of the upper edges in the correct sequence to the top and that it is not twisted. Then using strong sewing thread or dental floss, stitch each corner firmly in place onto the top section. Insert the first batten into the opposite corner pockets through the loop at the top of the seam on the panels. Then put the

second one in place above it and also through the loop. (The rods should fit fairly tightly, so you may have to bend the second one to fit into the pocket.)

Now all that remains is to decide on how to fasten the scoop to the hatch. The easiest method is to screw a snap-stud into each corner of the hatch opening, and insert the female half of the snap into the hem of the bottom outer corner of each panel. (Fig 167)

If this method does not work, a small screw or saddle-eye can be fitted to the cabin ceiling just inside each corner of the hatch, and the scoop fastened to these with a short length of cord through a grommet at each bottom corner of the panels.

Fasten a halyard to the webbing loop at the centre of the top, take up the tension until all four sides are evenly stretched (it may be necessary to tie a line forward to the forestay to hold it out) and go below to enjoy the cooling breeze.

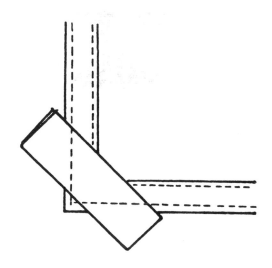

**Fig 166**

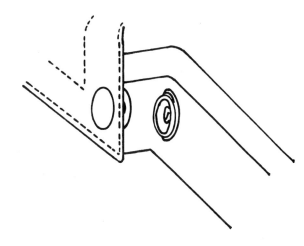

**Fig 167**

# Insect Screens

*What you will need*

Netting – Mosquito, garden or nylon netting

### Companionway Screen
1 length of light wooden batten (3cm wide by 5mm thick)
1 length of heavier wooden batten (3cm wide by 1cm thick)
2 saddle-eyes
5mm shock-cord
2 hooks

Insects can often spoil the pleasure of life aboard, especially the biting variety such as mosquitos or even worse, hornets. There are of course various methods to keep them at bay by the use of sprays, smoke and other devices, but most of these have a down-side being smelly and anti-social.

An alternative is to fit screens to hatches, ports and the companionway. The screens allow for the passage of cooling air and have the added advantage of offering privacy below if you are moored stern-to in a marina.

The simplest method of making an easy-access, removable screen for the companionway (which will take minimal stowage space when not in use) is to use cross-battens over the hatch openings to stop the net sagging and a heavier batten at the lower edge to hold the screen in place.

Measure the hatch opening and the depth and width of the doors or washboards. Cut the netting to run in a single length from the front of the hatch (when fully open) to the lower edge of the doors, adding 4cm to each side and 4cm at the lower edge. (Fig 168)

Cut two strips of sail tape the length of the sides, fold them in half and slot one over each side of the net, machining down the inner and outer edges. Trim off any excess at the ends.

Mark a line 1cm inside the upper and lower edges and stitch a strip of 5mm sail-tape to each line. Turn the tape over the cut edges of the net

*This companionway insect screen is effective and allows easy access to the interior of the boat.*

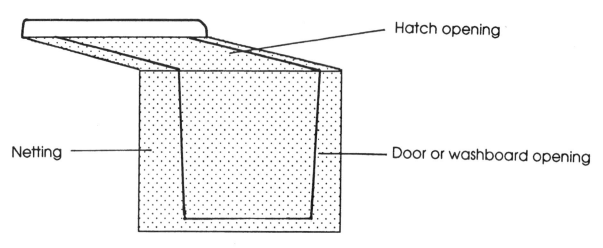

**Fig 168**

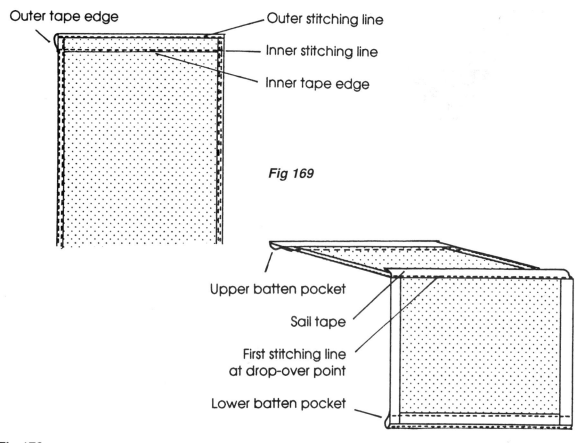

Outer tape edge

Outer stitching line

Inner stitching line

Inner tape edge

*Fig 169*

Upper batten pocket

Sail tape

First stitching line
at drop-over point

Lower batten pocket

*Fig 170*

and sew it down, reinforcing each end by revers-ing the stitching. This will give the forward (top) and the lower batten pockets. (Fig 169)

Lay the screen over the hatch and door aper-ture and mark the sides at the drop-over point. Draw a line between these points (on the outside of the netting) and machine down a strip of sail-tape to the line, with the free edge of the tape facing forward. (Fig 170)

Cut the tape ends with a hot-knife or soldering iron (or turn them under) to match the sides. Put a batten in place under the tape, which should then be pinned over onto the netting so that the screen base will lie flat. (Fig 171)

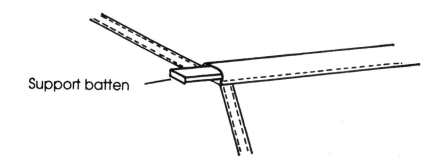

Support batten

*Fig 171*

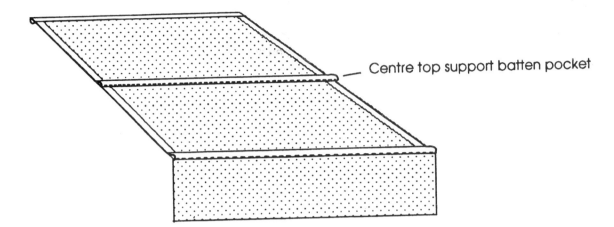

Centre top support batten pocket

**Fig 172**

Machine along the pinned edge, reversing the stitching at each end. At the centre of the hatch, between the two pockets, stitch another strip of tape for an extra cross-support pocket to stop the screen sagging. (Fig 172)

To attach the screen, fasten a saddle-eye at each side of the hatch cover. Drill a hole at each end of the forward batten, slightly inside the measurement between the saddle-eyes, and pass a short length of 5mm shock-cord through each end, stitching the short end around the batten to the longer length. (Fig 173)

Thread the longer end through a nylon hook, and after adjusting the tension on the shock-cord

(so that the batten is held tightly against the hatch) knot it and cut off any surplus.

To prevent the battens from slipping out of the pockets, put a couple of cross-stitches at each end. (Fig 174)

Once the screen is hooked onto each side of the hatch, the two other top battens will lie across the hatch surround to hold it in place, while the heavier batten at the lower edge will prevent it from flying out. It is possible to fasten the lower edges, but this limits the ease of entry and exit.

To stow the screen, simply roll it up. A tubular bag with a drawstring can be made to prevent the netting becoming snagged.

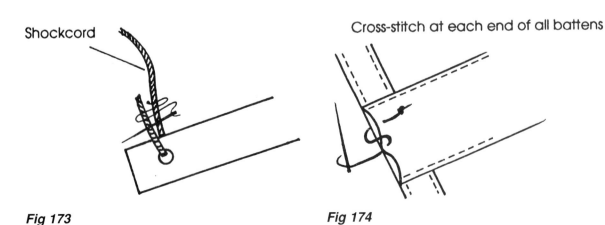

Shockcord

Cross-stitch at each end of all battens

**Fig 173**

**Fig 174**

## Hatch Screen

*What you will need*

4 – 8 snap-studs
3mm shock-cord

For a deck hatch screen, measure the opening, add 2cm to each side, and after cutting the net to these measurements, edge it with 5mm sail-tape in one length all round, sewn only on the inner edge, and leaving a gap at the centre of one long edge. (Fig 175)

At each corner fix a snap-stud (leaving enough room to run a length of 3mm shock-cord around the outer edge). Before inserting the shock-cord, mark the position of the other halves of the snaps and screw them in place. Then thread the shock-cord through the hem, tension it just enough to hold the screen close to the hatch and oversew the ends together. Machine the last piece of the hem into place, stretching the shock-cord as you sew.

It is also possible to fasten the hatch screen with stitched-on Velcro, but this means glueing the other half to the hatch surround, which looks unattractive when the screen is not in use.

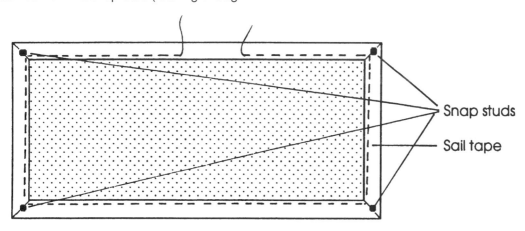

Snap studs

Sail tape

*Fig 175*

# Chart Protectors

*What you will need*

Clear plastic window material
Snap-studs or Velcro strips
Narrow webbing or bias tape

Charts are essential on all cruising yachts but being made of paper they can be easily damaged. Even on the chart table, sea-water dripping off oilskins or a spilled cup of coffee can often obliterate that one part of the chart that is essential. Also, when any courses, bearings and positions are marked, the subsequent erasure will rub the surface clear of print, especially when damp. Since charts are now a considerable expense it is well worth trying to protect them to prolong their life.

A sheet of clear plastic window material, as used for spray-hoods and tell-tale windows, cut to the exact size of the chart table ( up to the hinge if it has a lifting top) can provide the answer. A chinagraph pencil can be used to mark navigational references on the plastic, rather than on the chart paper itself. It is easily erased with a

*A chart shown beneath a clear plastic protective overlay.*

damp cloth when charts are changed or the information becomes redundant.

The only likely damage that may occur is when using dividers, when a strong prick could pierce the plastic and allow liquid to creep through the surface. This is altogether better, however, than leaving the entire chart face open to the abuse of sea-water, coffee and the multitude of other substances that always seem to arrive on the chart table.

The clear plastic should be attached firmly to the table by either snap studs at the corners and mid-points along all but the bottom sides or thin strips of Velcro. An important point to consider is that the chart should remain in the same position when it is being used for navigation. (Imagine the consequences if a chart was to slip a couple of inches under the plastic film upon which you had laid off courses and positions!) If there is any likelihood of the chart moving, use a product such as Blu-Tack that can be removed without defacing

the chart and yet will keep it in its original position. A sensible idea is to draw registration marks on the chart edges and also the plastic face, so that you can check to see if anything has shifted and if it has, you can then re-position the chart to its original position. (Fig 176)

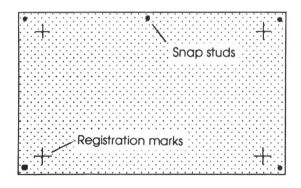

**Fig 176**

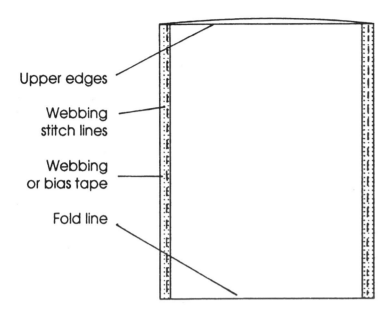

Upper edges

Webbing
stitch lines

Webbing
or bias tape

Fold line

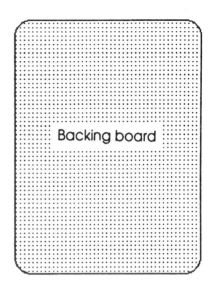

Backing board

***Fig 177***

When piloting in confined waters that are new to the navigator, it is quite important to be able to use a chart in the cockpit. If there is any wind, spray or rain about the situation becomes almost impossible and you can be sure that the chart will be damaged. Here is an idea that allows the use of a chart in the cockpit that will keep it dry, unmarked and unlikely to take to the air.

Cut a piece of 2–3 cm thick plywood or chipboard to the height of the chart and one third of the width. Round off the top and bottom edges to prevent the chart creasing. Cut a piece of clear plastic window material to twice the height of the board plus 14cm and 10cm more than the width. Fold it in half, matching the upper edges and sew the sides together and edge them with webbing or bias strips. (Fig 177)

At the centre of the upper open end, stitch a short length of Velcro to hold the chart in place. (Fig 178)

Roll the chart round the backing board with the required chart area uppermost, and slip it into the protective sleeve. By using this method you will be able to view two-thirds of the chart face at a glance by turning the sleeve over and will have a firm base upon which to lay off bearings and other navigational workings.

Velcro

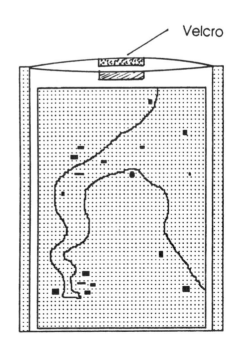

***Fig 178***

# Hanger Pockets

*What you will need*

PVC, canvas or acrylic – for the backing
The same materials or window material for the pockets
Turn-buttons
Thread, pins, tailor's chalk, straight-edge and measure

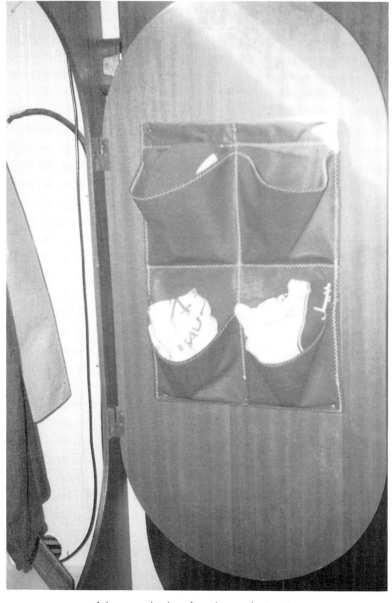

*A hanger locker for shoes, hats etc.*

114

It is always difficult to find sufficient stowage aboard a cruising yacht. Items that are seldom used tend to get buried at the bottom of lockers and drawers and when required, usually in a rush, the ensuing upheaval does not make for an orderly life. A simple solution is to fit hanger pockets, which can be made to fit any suitable space and to hold a variety of objects.

For example, a hanger pocket to hold engine repair tools and spares could be fixed to the back of the engine room door; another for spare flashlights and batteries onto the quarter-berth bulkhead; spare winch handles and bilge-pump handles could be stowed on the inside of the cockpit locker – with a little imagination you will find space for almost everything aboard.

The size of the hanging pocket will depend on the dimensions of the available space. If it is to be fitted to the back of the engine-room door or a hanging-locker door, you should allow 10cm clearance on the sides and 15cm at top and bottom.

You must first decide what is to be stowed and where. If the hanger pocket is to go on the inside of a locker door to hold clothing or shoes, the pocket backing size is not so critical. If it is designed to hold tools, the more secure and yet visible and accessible these are, the better.

Any hanger pocket will require a PVC, canvas or acrylic backing and for the pockets themselves, either the same material or clear plastic window material. If it is to be used for clothes, then canvas or acrylic is preferable; if it is to hold tools, PVC as a backing and clear plastic pockets will prove ideal as it is easy to wipe clean of oil and grease, will not be harmed by oil sprayed to prevent rust and finally, will allow you to spot the right tool quickly.

First measure the space that the hanger locker will occupy and subtract 10cm from each side and 15cm at top and bottom. This will be the finished measurement of the backing , so you will need to add 3cm all round for the hem. Turn over the hem and stitch it down (inner and outer edge). For a model that is to hold heavy tools it is better to leave the upper hem unstitched so that a support batten can be inserted. (Fig 179)

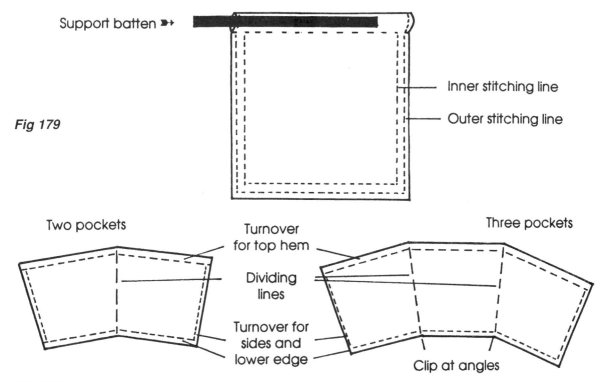

Support batten ➤

Inner stitching line

Outer stitching line

*Fig 179*

Two pockets

Turnover for top hem

Dividing lines

Turnover for sides and lower edge

Three pockets

Clip at angles

*Fig 180*

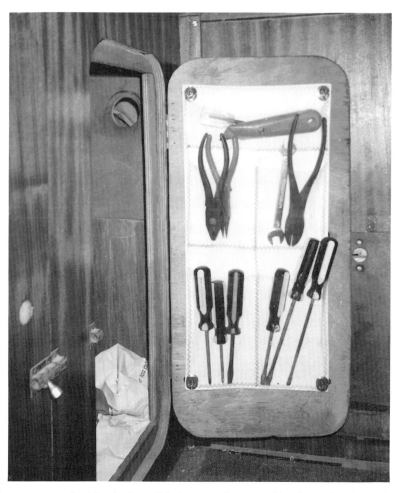

*It is easy to select tools from this hanger locker with clear plastic pockets.*

Decide what the pockets are to hold, to determine the individual pocket sizes. In the photo (where the pockets are to hold clothing, deck shoes etc) the upper pocket measurement is 25% wider than its backing segment and two-thirds of the height, while the lower edge matches the width exactly (plus 1cm turnover all round). To make the pockets gape open evenly, they should be cut from one piece at an angle in the centre.

Measure the width of the backing, divide it in half (or thirds if you want to put three pockets on each level) and add 25% to each top edge of each pocket, remembering to allow for the turnover all round. (If you are using clear plastic you will not need turnovers.) The pockets should now resemble Fig 180.

Turn over the upper edge and machine it down

(Not plastic), then press the sides and lower edge over, clipping the lower edge so that the cloth will lie flat.

To position the pockets, fold the backing in half lengthwise, and across, and mark the creases with chalk. (This is if you want two pockets per level; if you plan on three, fold it in thirds on the length.) These vertical lines are the guide-lines for the division between each pocket.

Pin or stick each set of pockets to the backing cloth, matching lower and side edges to the chalk lines, and the dividing lines to the vertical marks. (Fig 180). Stitch first along the lower edge of each set of pockets, then along the vertical marks, reinforcing the stitching at the upper edges. (see photo.)

To fasten the hanger pocket in place, use

either turn-button or 'Liftadot') fasteners (both of which have a surface fastening that can be screwed securely to wood or fibreglass) if you want the hanger pocket to be removable for washing or to enable you to get at the varnish behind it.

If you decide to use a support batten in the upper hem, cut it slightly less than the width to allow space for the eyelets in the cloth at each end.

The number of fasteners will depend on the finished size and the weight of the contents.

Normally one at each corner will be sufficient, but if it is designed to hold heavy tools it should have an extra one half-way on each side (and possibly a screw with a cup washer through the centre of the support batten).

When the hanger pocket is completed, fasten it to the bulkhead etc., with masking tape at each corner, and mark the centre points of the surface fittings through the holes, using a felt-tip or a spike. Position each fitting and screw them into place. Snap the hanger pocket on and load it up.

# Lee Cloths

*What you will need*

Acrylic or canvas material
No 1 grommets
Narrow strips of plywood or metal (stainless-steel or aluminium)
4mm line
Tailor's chalk, pins, measure, straight-edge, thread and scissors

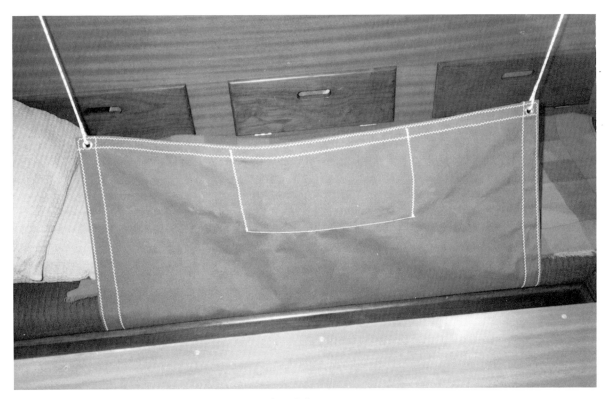

*A lee cloth provides a comfortable and safe berth in a seaway.*

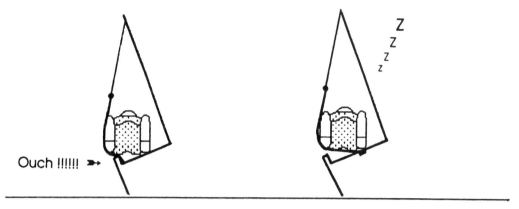

Ouch !!!!!! ➤+

**Lee cloth fixed to edge of bunk**          **Lee cloth fixed towards the berth's centre**

*Fig 181*

Imagine the sleeping mariner, comfortably wedged in his leeward berth, snoring contentedly as the boat beats steadily to windward. Alas, he fails to hear the helmsman's cry of 'Ready About'. As the boat turns and the sails fill on her new tack, she heels gracefully over – but what is all the commotion below?

You can visualise our mariner, now fully awake and nursing several bruises, trying to restore some order from the debris of scattered cushions, clothing and pillows. This is of course why lee cloths are vital when sailing on a passage where sleep will be required by the crew.

Most cruising yachts utilise the saloon settees as berths and it is usually these that are favoured whilst off-watch crews are sleeping. There is less movement than in the forepeak and the quarter berth is often aft of the chart-table and either the domain of the navigator alone or is left free so that others may occupy that space to make navigational checks or listen-in to the VHF. Therefore the settee berths must be made safe and comfortable whether they are to windward or leeward as the boat sails along.

Lee-cloths can be secured along the bottom, to the upper inside edge of the berth furniture that stands proud to keep the settee cushion in position. A better method, especially if you are likely to be making longer offshore passages, is to make the securing point between one-third and a half-way into the centre of the berth's width. (Fig

181) This means that it is actually beneath the occupant and when being used to windward, when the weight of the sleeping mariner is being supported mainly by the cloth, it will assume a curve that prevents buttocks and backs resting against the sharper corners of a right angled join between lee-cloth and bunk edge. It is more comfortable and more secure. There may, however be a problem in using this system if the top of the berth, below the cushion, has been cut and has lids that allow access to storage below the bunk.

Cut a rectangle of material two-thirds the length of the berth, plus 10cm. If the cloth is to be secured at its bottom on the bunk edge, measure 60cm width; if you are to position it towards the centre of the bunks width as recommended, add that extra distance to the 60cm width. (If using the 60cm width, it may be possible to buy acrylic in 120cm widths, thus allowing two lee-cloths to be cut from one length. Use a hot-knife to cut it.) Turn over 5cm on the two short sides and one long edge. Using a zig-zag stitch, sew down first the inner and then the outer edge. Then turn over the other long edge 5cm and stitch the inner edge only, reinforcing each end. (This hem will take the fastening batten.) (Fig 182)

It is a practical idea to sew a pocket or two on the inner side, to hold a book, spectacles etc. The main pocket should be (finished size) no more than 20cm deep from the top edge of the leecloth, so that it is clear of the sleeping body.

For the larger pocket, cut a piece of material 42cm long at the top edge and 38cm long at the bottom edge, by 23cm wide. Turn over 2cm at the top edge and stitch the hem. For a smaller pocket to fit on the inside, cut a rectangle of cloth 15cm long by 6cm wide, turn over 1cm at the top(long) edge and sew the hem. (Fig 183)

Turn over 5 mm on the short sides and the lower edge of the mini-pocket, and, matching the upper edges of both pockets, with the wrong sides together, pin and straight-line stitch the smaller one to the larger, towards the end where the head will lie. Draw a line 20.5cm down from the upper edge of the lee-cloth at the head end, 26cm long. (This is the marking for the lower edge of the big pocket.) At right-angles to this, draw a line at each end to the top of the lee-cloth as a guide for the pocket sides. (These marks to be on the inner side of the cloth.)

Turn over 5 mm on the short sides and lower edge of the large pocket, pin the lower edge to the line and match the sides to the side lines. (The pocket will gape open at the top, so that it will not stretch the lee-cloth when books etc. are put in it and will not crush spectacles when in the mini-pocket.)

Sew round the edges, using one or two lines of zig-zag stitching close together, and reinforcing the top corners by reversing the stitching. (Fig 184)

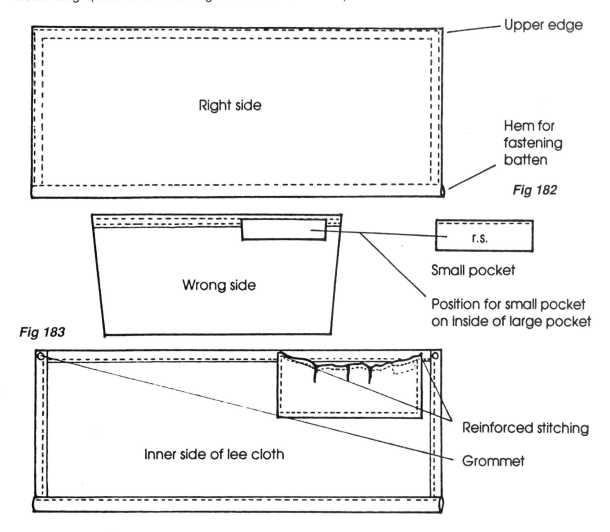

Upper edge

Right side

Hem for fastening batten

Fig 182

Wrong side

r.s.

Small pocket

Position for small pocket on inside of large pocket

Fig 183

Inner side of lee cloth

Reinforced stitching

Grommet

Fig 184

At the two upper corners of the lee-cloth, put in a No 1 grommet to hold the lines.

For the support batten at the lower edge, a strip of 2cm wide aluminium, stainless-steel or thin plywood should be cut to the length of the lee-cloth and the edges sanded off or smoothed. Drill holes at 15cm distances, lay the batten on the hem (inner side) and mark the hole positions.

Slide the batten into the hem; using a small spike, check that the marks match the drilled holes and position the centre of the lee-cloth to the centre of the bunk facing. If fastening to the front of the bunk, fix it as low as possible, so that when not in use, the lee-cloth will fold flat under the settee cushion. If securing it further towards the centre of the bunkboard, ensure that the batten is parallel to the bunk side. To fasten the batten, use small countersink screws through cup washers, to avoid damage to the cushion covers. (Fig 185)

Screw a saddle-eye onto the trim (if it is solid enough) at either end, or onto the bulkhead fore and aft, to attach the lee-cloth corner lines. The lines should be fastened to the cloth by stitching or seizing.

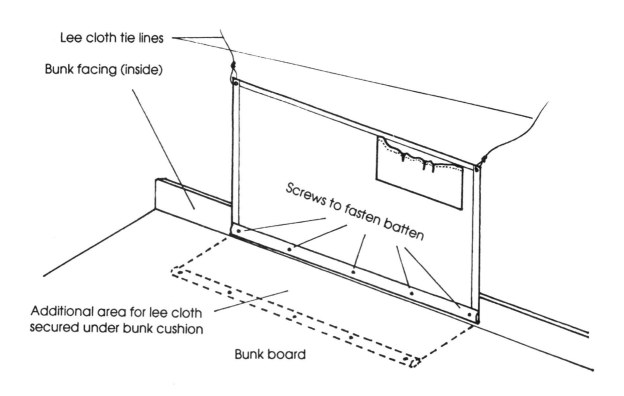

Lee cloth tie lines

Bunk facing (inside)

Screws to fasten batten

Additional area for lee cloth secured under bunk cushion

Bunk board

**Fig 185**

# Outboard-engine Covers

*What you will need*

UV-resistant material
Waterproof material
3mm cord
2.5cm webbing

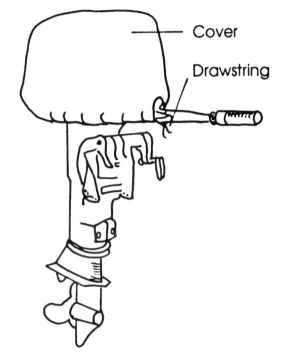

An outboard-engine is a difficult piece of equipment to stow below or in cockpit lockers. Many boats carry them clamped onto the pushpit, a sensible place where it is out of the way and where any petrol fumes are unlikely to cause problems. The engine itself does however, need protection from the elements and a suitable cover can stop the salt-water environment doing too much damage. (Fig 186)

To obtain the basic design measurements, take the dimensions of the engine-case by first of all measuring loosely around the base and then around the upper part to include the steering arm and starter handle. Take the larger of the measurements and halve it. (A) Then measure from underneath, over the top at the aft end (B) and the forward end (C). (Fig 187)

**Fig 186**

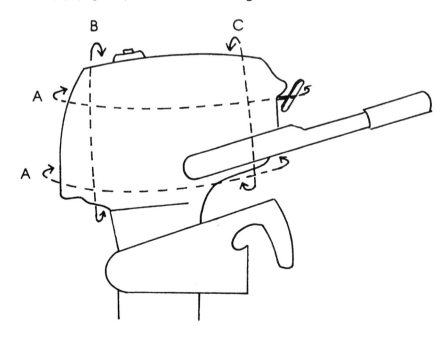

**Fig 187**

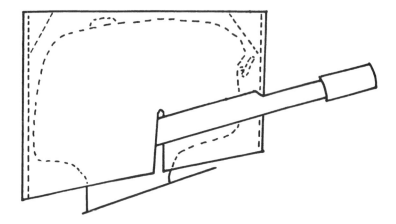

**Fig 188**

If the width of the cloth is B or less, cut the length of the longest half A, and with the selvedges together, crease along the fold, matching the cut edges; then stitch them down. Slip the cover over the engine casing and slit the cloth so that the steering arm protrudes.

Pinch the corners in to follow the profile, pin them and stitch along these lines. (Fig 188)

To square off the corners, match the seams at the top centre crease and pin across each corner; stitch along these lines and trim off the excess material 1cm from the stitching. (Fig 189)

For the steering arm cut out, trim the top into a smooth curve, slightly wider than the handle and strengthen the opening with a length of webbing folded in half and stitched over the raw edge. (Fig 190)

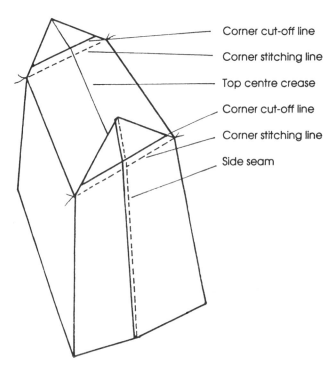

Corner cut-off line
Corner stitching line
Top centre crease
Corner cut-off line
Corner stitching line
Side seam

**Fig 189**

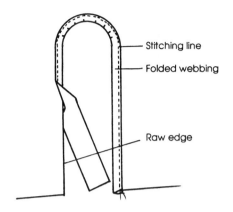

- Stitching line
- Folded webbing
- Raw edge

**Fig 190**

Trim off the excess webbing level with the lower edge and mark the hem fold 3cm up. Crease along this line and zig-zag stitch along the upper (cut) edge only, reversing the stitching over the webbing. Run a drawstring through the hem, leaving protruding at each side of the handle cut out. Stitch the cord in place at the centre back to prevent it pulling out.

Fit the cover over the outboard and pull the drawstring tight under the handle before tying it with a slip hitch. Then either tuck the ends inside or tie them round the handle to ensure that the cover cannot blow off. (Fig 186)

# Liferaft – Stowage and Covers

*What you will need*

4 eye-bolts
Flexible stainless-steel wire
Padlock
UV-proof fabric
3mm leechline or shock-cord and line
No 1 grommets
Tape measure, tailor's chalk and straight edge

The most common position for a liferaft to be stowed is on deck, often on the coachroof between the companionway hatch and the mast. Since these items are pretty bulky and certainly heavy, it is quite probable that you will leave it there permanently whilst cruising. The trouble is, that since they are expensive pieces of kit, they often attract the attention of unscrupulous eyes once your back is turned.

The only solution is to make them as secure as possible and difficult to remove when you are taking a run ashore and leaving the boat unattended. If you have a liferaft that is contained within a plastic or fibreglass case and it is stowed on wooden chocks, it can be made too difficult to move surreptitiously and will therefore deter the average petty criminal.

Drill two holes through the lower ends of both chocks and fit eye-bolts with the eyes outward. The nuts will be very difficult to tamper with when the liferaft is on the chocks. (Fig 191)

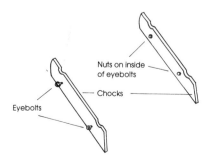

Nuts on inside of eyebolts
Chocks
Eyebolts

**Fig 191**

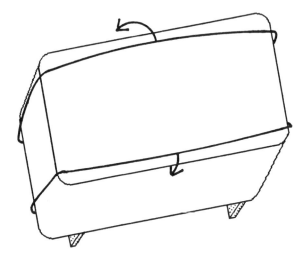

**Fig 192**

With the raft resting in position on the chocks, tie a light line through the aft eye-bolt at one side, pass it over the top of the raft and down through the opposite eye. Pull it taut over the raft, then slacken it just enough to slip over the case to the deck. Mark where it passes through each eye-bolt; these will be the outer ends of the wire strop. Do the same for the forward eye-bolts. (Fig 192)

Cut two lengths of flexible stainless-steel wire (4–6mm) to the same measurement from mark to mark, plus 5cm at each end to allow for a swage. Transfer the outer end marks from the cord to the wire, 5cm in from each end. At one end of each wire, thread a swage over, pass the wire through the fore and aft eye-bolts at one side, slide the swages on and fasten them. (If you do not have a swaging machine, a cold chisel and hammer will hold it in place.)

Before swaging the wires through the opposite eye-bolts, check that the lengths are correct (after sliding the swage down the wire) crease or mark the point where they pass through. Remove the raft and fit the swages.

Replace the raft and pull the two wires up over it; they should come towards each other at the centre leaving a gap of about 10–20cm. Tie them together at this point. Measure from the centre of the aft wire, over the forward wire and round under the raft to the centre of the forward wire. This is the finished length of the security strop. Cut a piece of wire to this length plus 5cm for

swaging and form an eye round the aft wire. (Fig 193)

To avoid the wire damaging the raft, slide it through a length of rubber or plastic pipe, allowing the wire to protrude for the eye at the other end. This should just touch the centre of the forward wire. Form the eye, and use an all-brass or stainless-steel padlock to fasten it to the forward cross wire. (Fig 194)

For a seagoing lashing, remove the padlock and coil the security strop under the raft. Lash the two cross wires together with a slip knot using a short length of strong cord. The raft will be firmly held in place, but easy to launch if necessary.

Do remember to remove the padlock when you put to sea. The consequences of not having done so in an emergency are obvious.

A valise-packed liferaft can be secured with a single wire by passing the wire though the handles and around a substantial part of the boat and then joined with a padlock

**Fig 193**

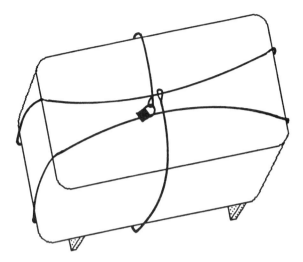

*Fig 194*

## Liferaft Covers

A cover will protect a liferaft from the relentless UV onslaught found in the lower latitudes. Even a canister-type raft will suffer, in particular the seal, so a quick-release cover is worth considerable thought to preserve the life of this expensive article.

The cover should be long enough all round to gather just under the lower curve, or to where the raft rests on its chocks. For the amount of material, measure from deck to deck over the width of the canister and add 6cm for the hem.

Now measure the length of one long and one short side at the fattest part and add 4cm. Cut a rectangle of cloth to these measurements. (The normal width of UV-resistant material should be enough to cover most rafts from fore to aft; if not, add a strip at one lower edge where the stitching will not be too exposed to the sun.) Fold the material in half along the width and straight-stitch down the sides, creasing the upper fold. (Fig 195)

Press the seams open and crease the corners so that the fold lines lie to the stitching (seam) lines. (Fig 196)

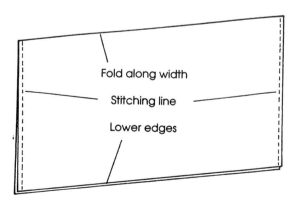

Fold along width

Stitching line

Lower edges

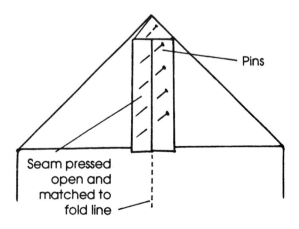

Pins

Seam pressed open and matched to fold line

*Fig 195*

*Fig 196*

Measure the upper short side of the canister and mark this length across the corner, using the seam/fold at the centre as a half-way mark.

Stitch along this line, curving each end downwards slightly to give a rounded corner effect. Tie off each end (or back-stitch over) and trim off the excess material 1cm inside the stitching line, using a hot-knife to seal it. (Fig 197)

Fit the cover over the canister and mark it at each point where it touches the chocks. Lay it flat and draw a line between each mark. This will be the turnover line for the hem. Draw another line 3cm down and cut off any excess with a hot-knife.

To fasten the cover in place, the two most practical methods are:

1) A length of shock-cord run through the hem, tensioned to gather the cover underneath. For this you will need to stitch around the hem, leaving a small gap to thread the shock-cord through before tensioning it and either tying the ends together or overlapping and stitching them. Then finish off the last part of the hem and at the centre of each long side put a grommet just above the shock-cord for a securing line under the raft.

2) A drawstring. For this insert two grommets 3cm apart just above the hem crease at the centre of one long side. Then turn the hem to the inside and sew it down with two close lines of zig-zag stitching (one as close as possible to the cutting edge, and the second just inside this). Run a length of 3mm leechline through the grommet, round the hem and out through the other grommet and knot the ends securely together, leaving about 20cm protruding, to allow for the slip-hitch once the tension is taken up round the lower edge of the raft – or, put a grommet at the opposite centre (long side) and allow enough spare cord to pass under the raft and tie through it.

Whichever method you choose, it must be secure and instantly releasable.

## Valise-packed liferaft

Avon recommend that valise-packed liferafts are stowed in an easily accessed cockpit locker, as the valise is laced around the raft and if this is exposed to the elements, rain or sea-water can

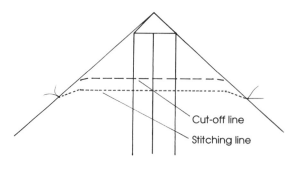

*Fig 197*

find its way through the folds onto the raft, which may result in deterioration and possibly prevent the raft functioning correctly.

However if you are short of locker space and have to stow the raft on deck, a water-proof UV-resistant cover should provide adequate protection.

For the main body of the cover, measure the length of the valise (A) and from deck to deck over the top (B). (Fig 198)

Cut a rectangle to this size adding 2cm to A for the seam allowance and 6cm on B for the hem turnover. Mark the centres on B.

Measure the width and height from the deck to top at one end, and cut the two U-shaped pieces

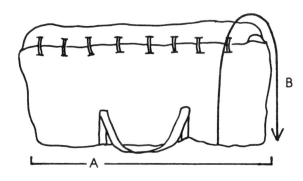

*Fig 198*

to this size (plus 2cm on the width and 4cm on the height). (Fig 199)

Mark the bottom of the curve at the centre and pin it to the centre mark of the rectangle. Clipping the straight edges, match them to the curve and straight-line stitch 1cm inside. (Fig 200)

Press the seam allowance to the rectangle, and from the outside, zig-zag stitch close to the join for a neater, stronger finish. (Fig 201)

Do the same at the other end, then try the cover over the valise. Mark the hem turnover line where it touches the deck, turn the excess in and crease it along the line.

At the centre front, insert two grommets 5cm apart, just above the crease, before zig-zagging the hem (on the inner edge only). Thread a length of 3mm cord through the hem with the free ends out through the grommets. When both ends are equal, put a couple of hand stitches through the material and the cord at the opposite side to prevent the cord pulling out. The drawstring, when pulled tight, will gather the lower edges of the cover round the valise and prevent it blowing off. Tie the free ends in a quick-release knot and tuck them inside out of the way.

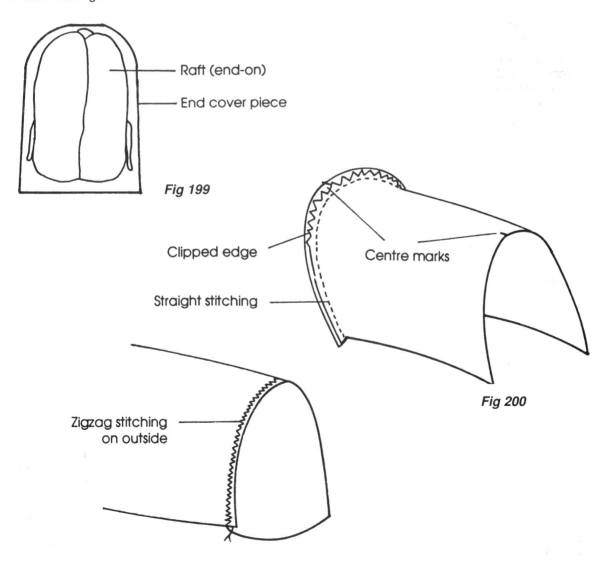

Raft (end-on)

End cover piece

**Fig 199**

Clipped edge

Centre marks

Straight stitching

**Fig 200**

Zigzag stitching on outside

**Fig 201**

# Replacing Windows in a Spray-hood

*What you will need*

Clear window material
Double-sided tape

The life-span of clear flexible plastic windows is generally less than the material surrounding them. This can depend on several factors, however; the quality of the window material, the way it is treated and the consideration of your neighbours – to name but three.

The sailmaker's supplier Bainbridge make window material in several different grades, thicknesses and prices. The most expensive being in sheet form, UV-resistant and very flexible. Most cover makers will install this top-grade if you specify it and are willing to pay the increase in price. It is unlikely that you will find it in a small service loft unless it is specially ordered in advance.

The average window has a life-span of two to five years, depending on usage and how carefully you look after them. They should never be creased or stepped on. When you fold down a spray-hood, lay a rolled up towel along the fold to protect the curve. If you moor in a working marina, where you may be unlucky enough to

have a neighbouring boat owner who wants to grind-off his steel deck or gas bottle, or use a wire-brush on a high-speed drill, for the sake of your spray-hood (and your boat) ask for enough warning to allow you to remove the hood (or preferably your boat). Metal filings or grindings will adhere to almost anything, and though they may not be noticed at first, dampness will soon bring out rust spots. On a fibreglass deck these can be removed, but the particles will embed themselves into clear plastic, leaving you with no alternative but to replace all the windows.

If the hood is left up when not in use, outside protection against the sun can be achieved with snap on curtains. (Ask the maker for the 'cut outs' – which, in most cases you have paid for anyway) – and add an edging all round to overlap the window. This will allow room to put in snap-studs at each corner and midway on each long side (top and bottom) or to stitch a short length of Velcro at the upper and lower edges. (Fig 202)

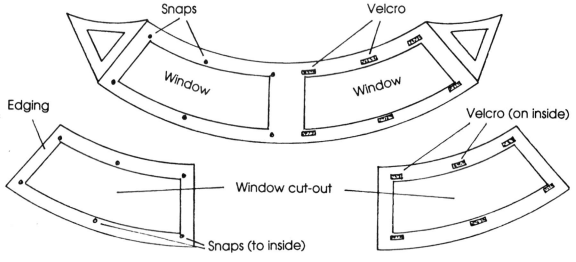

**Fig 202**

128

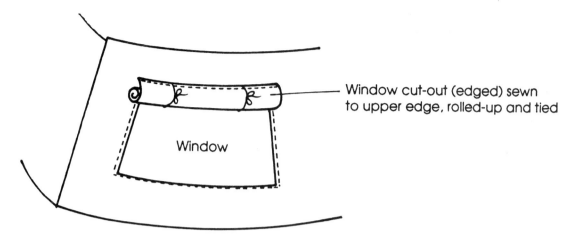

Window cut-out (edged) sewn to upper edge, rolled-up and tied

Window

**Fig 203**

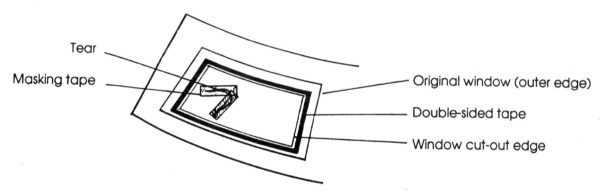

Tear

Masking tape

Original window (outer edge)

Double-sided tape

Window cut-out edge

**Fig 204**

Or you could ask the maker to do the edging for you, and to stitch the upper edge to the cover with ties to hold it up when the curtain is rolled up. (Fig 203)

There are advantages and disadvantage to this method. The main advantage is because it is there, you are more likely to use it, when the sun gets in your eyes or you need some privacy; the disadvantages – extra stitching holes in the cover and the chance of wind or sea tearing it off.

If the windows have become opaque or yellowed in the sun (or badly discoloured by rubbing against the frame), they are likely to be brittle and ready to crack. At this point, they should be replaced. (Easier to do before they tear.)

If they are already cracked or torn, fix them to the original shape with masking tape on both sides, as it is much easier to use the old one for a pattern.

On the inside, run a strip of double-sided tape around the edge, just inside the cut edge of the cloth. (Fig 204)

Lay the window flat, with the inside uppermost, and if necessary fasten it down (through the seams) with push-pins. Lay the new window on top, push-pinned in place at three corners. Starting at the fourth corner, pull off the paper backing on the double-sided tape along and down as far as the next pins, pressing the window down as you go. As you reach one corner, remove the pin, peel off the paper and press down until you reach the next corner. When the window is stuck in place all round, carefully trim off the surplus just outside the original window edging, turn the cover over and stitch all round the cover cut out (without allowing the needle to pierce the window). Sew round again 1cm outside this, and turn the cover over again so that the new window lies on old newspaper or a towel to prevent scratching.

With a pair of fine scissors, snip through the old window into a corner and cut it carefully out round the original cover cut out, leaving only the new window showing.

(This is a far more accurate method than unpicking the old window first and then having to guess at the stretch and curves of the material.)

If your new window material is not wide or long enough to re-do the window in one piece, it can be joined at the centre. This will however create a weak point which should be reinforced by a strip of cover material (2cm wider than the joining seam) on each side of the window, extending over the upper and lower seaming lines. (Fig 205)

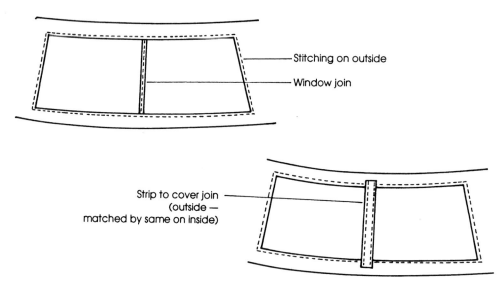

Stitching on outside

Window join

Strip to cover join (outside — matched by same on inside)

**Fig 205**

# Buttoned Cushions

*What you will need*

Buttons – domed 'shank' type
Button (or waxed) thread
Long darning needle

To add a professional look to your saloon cushions, consider buttoning them; this will ensure that the pattern, especially if striped or checked material, will lie straight at the edges and will also take out any slack in the fabric.

The length of the cushions will determine the number of buttons needed; though this is a matter of choice. For the average saloon, four buttons (evenly spaced on the centreline) should be enough for the long back cushions, and one on each short bulkhead cushion. Using tailor's chalk, mark each button's position on the backs, then match the seat buttons as closely in line with the backs as possible along the seat centre line. (The centres of the side seats may not line up with the button line on the long cushion, but the overall effect will be neater if the back and seat buttons match.) (Fig 206)

*Buttons draw the fabric taut over the cushions to give a more pleasing appearance.*

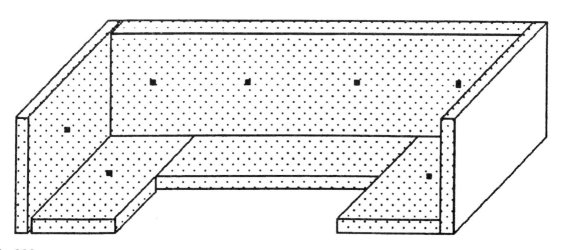

**Fig 206**

Since the saloon cushions covers need to be removable from time to time for washing or cleaning, it is worth applying them with a protective coating (eg Scotchgard™) before buttoning them – this will preserve the colour and enable dirt or spills to be easily wiped off.

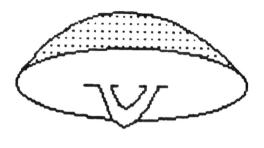

**Fig 207**

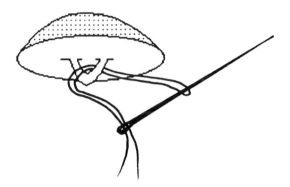

**Fig 208**

The buttons should be of the 'shank' type, with a domed head so that the thread does not show. (Fig 207)

If the cushions are reversible, use the same buttons on both sides.

Using a long darning needle, take a double length of heavy button thread (or light waxed twine) and pass both cut ends through the eye. Pass the needle through the shank of the upper button and back through the loop at the end of the thread. (Fig 208)

At each mark on the cushion, push the needle straight through at right-angles, checking that it emerges at the corresponding point on the other side, leaving the thread-ends dangling. When you are satisfied with the placement, turn the cushion over; divide each pair of threads, and pass them in opposite directions through the shank of the backing button. (Fig 209)

Pull up on the threads to give the required 'dip'

on the upper side of the cushion, wind the ends in opposite directions twice round the shank of the button, tie them off and cut the ends.

Once the buttons are marked and stitched for the first time, it is simple enough to remove them and replace them.

## Corner or Scatter Cushions

*What you will need*

Bags of 'minced' foam or kapok
Cotton or nylon liner material
Covering material
Zips

Cushions can enhance the interior of any boat, especially where a fabric ties together the woodwork, settee and curtains.

In the photo, the varnish is medium oak, the curtains are orange-gold and the settee cushions are dark blue/light blue stripe; so by choosing a fabric that contains these colours (either on a neutral – beige or cream – background, or on a completely contrasting one – such as red or black) your saloon can take on a completely new look.

The cushions can be made solely for use in the saloon, in which case a square shape (40 – 50cm each side) is best; or they can double as bunk pillows, which should measure 40 × 55cm.

Unless you have old cushions or pillows to recover, it is far cheaper to buy bags of 'minced'

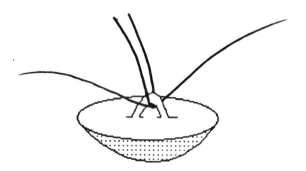

**Fig 209**

*Cushions can add contrast to a saloon's colour scheme.*

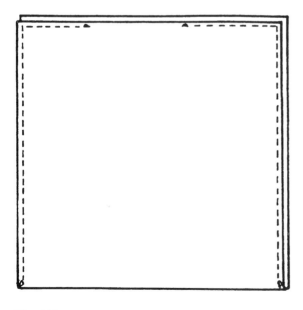

**Fig 210**

foam pieces or kapok and to make the inner liners from inexpensive cotton or nylon (or old sheets) to the required shape and size, than to buy ready-made ones.

Cut a strip twice the finished length, fold it in half and stitch down each side and part-way along the top edge, leaving a 20cm gap at the centre to allow for filling. (Fig 210)

Turn the liner the other way out and press it flat.

Whatever the stuffing you use, this is best done outside, in a sheltered place – and down-wind! (As inevitably some will get spilled.) Pack the stuffing well into each corner first, then fill the centre as tightly as possible. Pin the open edges together and oversew them closely.

For the outer fabric cover, cut two squares (or rectangles) to the same size as the inner cover plus 1cm all round. On the short edge of each half, fold the cloth under 1cm and sew in a zip (3–4cm shorter than the length leaving 1.5–2cm open at each end, and making sure that the folded edges meet so that the zip will not show. (Fig 211)

Turn the cover so that the right sides are together, pin the edges and machine round 1cm inside the cutting line on the other three sides, reinforcing the stitching at each end. (If you are using fabric that frays easily – loosely woven cloth – the covers will last longer if the cut edges are strengthened with a row of zig-zag stitching.)

Turn the cover right side out and press it flat; hand stitch the openings at each end of the zip on the fourth edge and stuff the liner cushion inside, matching the corners.

If you have made the square saloon cushions, they may look neater with a button through the centre on each side (to match buttons on the seat covers). However, if they are to double as pillows, this could be uncomfortable, so it is better to leave them unbuttoned. In this case, have loose-fitting pillowcases ready to slip on for night-time use.

If you want the cushions to stay in place while sailing, a strip of Velcro (the hooked side) can be sewn to the back. This will prevent them flying off the seats.

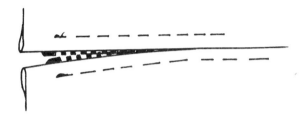

**Fig 211**

# Index